FASHIONING APPETITE

ARTS and TRADITIONS of the TABLE

Arts and Traditions of the Table: Perspectives on Culinary History
Albert Sonnenfeld, Series Editor

FASHIONING APPETITE

RESTAURANTS

AND THE

MAKING

OF

MODERN

IDENTITY

JOANNE FINKELSTEIN

COLUMBIA UNIVERSITY PRESS ❖ NEW YORK

Columbia University Press
Publishers Since 1893
New York   Chichester, West Sussex
cup.columbia.edu
Copyright © 2014 Joanne Finkelstein

First published by I.B.Tauris & Co. Ltd in the United Kingdom

Library of Congress Cataloging-in-Publication Data

Finkelstein, Joanne.
  Fashioning appetite : restaurants and the making of modern identity /
Joanne Finkelstein.
      pages cm — (Arts and traditions of the table : perspectives on
      culinary history)
  Follow-up to: Dining out : a sociology of modern manners. 1989.
  Includes bibliographical references and index.
  ISBN 978-0-231-16796-3 (cloth : alk. paper) — ISBN 978-0-231-53712-4
  (e-book)
  1. Restaurants—Social aspects. 2. Dinners and dining—Social aspects.
  3. Food—Social aspects. 4. Appetite—Social aspects. 5. Identity
  (Psychology) 6. Civilization, Western. 7. Civilization, Modern—1950–
  I. Finkelstein, Joanne. Dining out. II. Title.

    TX911.2.F56 2013
    647.95—dc23

                                                              2013019082

Columbia University Press books are printed on permanent and durable
acid-free paper.
This book is printed on paper with recycled content.
Printed in the UK

c 10 9 8 7 6 5 4 3 2 1

Jacket designed by Julia Kushnirsky.
Jacket image © Getty

Designed and typeset by 4word Ltd, Bristol, UK

CONTENTS

INTRODUCTION

Illusion is the first of all pleasures.

VOLTAIRE

Restaurants are ubiquitous. Every main street, village corner, commercial strip, shopping mall and scenic tourist outpost seems to have a food outlet of some kind. They vary in size, shape and quality from the mobile coffee canteen to the famously extravagant and opulent decor of the Michelin-starred restaurant that boasts an extensive menu, celebrity clientele and illustrious chef. The most common variety of restaurant in the affluent Western society is found on the local high street and neighborhood shopping mall where it is accepted as part of everyday life. As such, eating out can be seen as a simple transaction between the physical need for sustenance and commercial opportunity. At one level, this is so, and the history of early restaurants such as travelers' inns and urban chophouses supports this, but more interesting are questions about the importance of eating in public to our sense of being social. The questions explored in this book concern where we eat, with whom, how often, at what cost and why; these questions go beyond obvious commercialism to ask how the practice of dining out has been absorbed into our sense of everyday identity.

Restaurants are themselves interesting social spaces; their design, decor and internal operations provide insights into current cultural norms and aesthetic values. As platforms for much of our social activity, they offer a means for illustrating the importance we attach to displaying ourselves in public. Fashions in dining are constantly changing; once it was more common for a celebratory meal to take place in a restaurant with nineteenth-century decor – brocade chairs, heavy tables, chandeliers, snobbish waiters – the kind of decor found in New York's famous Delmonico's or Maxim's in Paris. Now, such an occasion might take place in a minimalist Japanese–French fusion restaurant where the decor is sleekly avant-garde with curiously shaped cutlery and seductively familiar staff, and a menu that offers exotic taste sensations. In short, styles of restaurant vary greatly, yet for all their variety of appearance, they function socially in much the same way. Irrespective of the rapid turnover in styles, restaurants provide a prismatic perspective on contemporary social habits and, in particular, the way we see ourselves as social actors participating in the public arena.

The restaurant is highly engineered; whether it is a self-servicing fast food outlet or the silver service of an elegant brasserie, it tacitly directs us to observe its protocols and act in a predictable manner. The new open public sphere of Western modernity and the changing nature of sociality are well illustrated through the history of the restaurant. The early coffee houses of London were liberal environments that encouraged experiments to take place such as talking across the social barriers. Individuals (although most commonly men) learned new ways to see and think about themselves and others. The early coffee houses and restaurants were schools of subjectivity, and in many ways they still function as such. Thus their ubiquity in the societies of the wealthy West can be explained in part by their effectiveness as social mirrors to human commerce that reflect and display our knowledge of conventional conduct. Restaurants – in all their variety – allow us to examine the dimensions of selfhood and identity that are disported in the public arena and come to be accepted as normal everyday modes of being in the world.

The preoccupation with food and eating outside the home is a telling feature of modern urban life that uncovers social practices at the core of our culture. The focus of this book is not directly on cuisine, or food styles, or celebrity chefs delivering the perfect meal, or influential food critics and commentators who can make or break a restaurant's reputation, but on the cultivation of the popular appetite for dining out itself. How has it happened that eating out has become so imbricated with our search for entertaining pleasures and self-expression; how has the private desire for novelty and amusement become so closely associated with the modern restaurant? The particular ways we have of thinking about ourselves and the world we live in are, of course, specific to political and economic conditions. However, understanding this conflu-ence of external circumstances with interior sensibilities is not part of our daily parlance, but is taken for granted as a normal way of acting. Yet these habits are embedded in the ever-shifting social conditions that fashion us; that have made us repositories of influences we are not always conscious of absorbing.

It may seem a long bow to draw a connection between the popularity of restaurants and the making of modern identity, and of how we think of ourselves as self-regulat-ing, autonomous individuals; however, there is a history of debate connecting the public and the private, the macroscopic and the microscopic, the interior sensibili-ties and the external context. The centrality of dining out in contemporary life positions the restaurant at the junction of these debates. Our personal habits and desires are constantly being cultivated as we inhabit shifting circumstances, and how we act may be seen as a local illustration of more abstract influences that exist at a remote structural level. Our search for love, happiness, amusement, success, and so on is an impetus that is constantly expressed through cultural forms. These states of being are reinforced on a daily basis; how and why we choose to act in accord with these normative imperatives contributes to a sense of identity. Pierre Bourdieu's (1984) study of the French middle classes is an example where the connections between the macroscopic and the microscopic, between the cultural and the individual, have been mapped in detail. However, the idea that we are in a state of constant invention has been resonating through centuries of Western culture. A legacy of Western thought is that the taken-for-granted social world is an artificial product of the imagination. We live in a world of arbitrary forms that have emerged from a range of possibilities, and when we recognize this, we understand better that our current views on the social function as a framework that allows us to see how such views have been constructed.

In 1714, Bernard Mandeville's satirical poem was published as *The Fable of the Bees* in which he described the connections between private interests and public benefit. The freedom of the upper classes to pursue their own comforts, to develop luxury tastes and private vices, eventually cascaded down into the lower classes who were employed to support these interests, and through commercial exchange provided a kind of wider social benefit. Mandeville proposed that the economic success of a society rested with this symbiotic exchange between private vice and public benefit; so the freedom to pursue personal desires by the wealthy and privileged created opportunities for others to gain some secondary benefit. As a consequence, the pursuit of convenience or natural selfishness or gratification (whatever it is called) was a key ingredient to broad-scale economic prosperity. This remains an interesting idea in the contemporary West where the entertainment industries that sell amusement and cultivate the desire for personal satisfaction are among the most lucrative and powerful forces in the global economy. The marketing of desire consequently produces a complex scaffolding of economic opportunity. Behind every whim to buy gluten-free bread, Illy coffee, a Burberry scarf or Doc Martens shoes, there is a long chain of commercial intelligence.

From about the eighteenth century, as more complex and elaborate social and economic environments developed with the emergence of mercantile capitalism, and the more formally administrated sphere of commerce, greater attention was paid to the fundamental sociological question of the nature of the relationship between the individual and society. The tension between the micro and macro levels in society has continued in a variety of forms into the contemporary era. If private vice or indulgence leads to public benefits, there is a question of whether this is the right and proper manner for a society to be organized. Should the benefits of private vice enjoyed by a small sector of society be permitted because they generate commerce and opportunities for others? Do these kinds of questions have any relevance to the contemporary practice of dining out engaged in by millions of people and not just a select few? The approach taken in this book is to focus on the pursuit of pleasure, entertainment and convenience as a form of conspicuous consumption, and to inquire whether the popularity of dining out provides a context in which to comment on the relationship between the private and public: between the immediate lived experiences of the individual and the authority of high-level abstract social values that find their expression through popular conventions and manners.

The practice of dining out is regarded as a form of emotion-work, and its widespread popularity suggests that it forms part of our personal constitution. Our appetites are fashioned from a variety of external influences that become blended into an identity that we use to organize our everyday desires. Thus the manner in which we act is not just about displaying a sense of individualism; it is also a means through which we grasp the significance of our position in the world and how we bridge the divide between ourselves and others. Our tastes in music, entertainment, beliefs and values give form and significance to our surroundings. Taking the popular practice of dining out as a vehicle for exploring the ways in which we occupy the social domain and interact with others gives insight into how we have constructed personal identity, and how important we think its expression. Defining the nature of our emotions, desires, satisfactions and appetites is not an endgame. These are not stable, measurable quantities; nonetheless, they do function as real propulsions and so become visible to us through action. In this sense, identity is what we do, how we perform and how we regard the reactions of others. Identity is not ours to imagine or think of as an essential core, but it is a product of our social habits. How we understand ourselves as modern and civilized, how we have cultivated the types of social exchanges that seem proper and conventional, and how we have developed our appetites and chosen to enact them in the public arena are the main preoccupations that frame this book. The popular practice of dining out is a means for exploring these concerns, as the restaurant itself is located squarely in the space between the private and public.

The early restaurant was a theater for spectacle, a place where the unexpected was welcomed. Its tolerance of the bawdy, lascivious, transgressive and boisterous meant that individuals learned to become increasingly tolerant of others and prepared to indulge their peculiarities. These social arenas put the individual on display; people could linger and be entertained by observing others as well as being a source of amusement themselves. The public domain became a stage for experimentation. The details of dress and deportment were decipherable signs of status and personal proclivities. Styled appearances made the manners of dissemblance more obvious, and thus the perception took hold that the social world is a theater where all human relations are continuously staged and engineered.

From these forerunners, we have understood the importance of how others see us. Our public demeanor is a clue to inner character; thus Lord Chesterfield, in 1741, famously advised his son that as he will be best known by his fashionable display of manners, he should cultivate them carefully. How we disport ourselves in public, how we choose to entertain ourselves and pursue novel forms of sociality, is regarded as evidence of our character; making our proclivities visible through the public pursuit of our tastes and pleasures has made the social domain a site of liberality and a laboratory for subjectivity, where the restaurant, in particular, has been instrumental in making this possible. How we have willingly agreed to act in these ways emerges from a long history of mercantilism, the growth of democratic institutions and the sociology of the city itself.

It is taken for granted now that every cosmopolitan city of the modern world will have a restaurant precinct or two – the iconic examples are London's Mayfair and Soho, Sydney's Darling Harbour, Melbourne's Lygon Street, Manhattan's Greenwich Village, the 5th and 8th arrondissements in Paris, and Tokyo's Ginza. These distinctive territories provide an arena where we disport ourselves publicly in search of pleasure and entertainment. Food retail more generally also supports a variety of commercial interests such as glossy cookbooks by celebrity chefs, fine dining trails through tourist areas of Provence, Tuscany, Tasmania and Scandinavia, reality television competitions for the discovery of the next master chef, mass advertising for the sale of elegant designer kitchenware for the home cook, and fame and some fortune for popular food critics writing in the broadcast media such as A.A. Gill, Cherry Ripe and Ruth Reichl. Changes to the modern family, shifting career households and irregular working hours have also meant that meals are less patterned, and the restaurant in its various forms has been marketed to respond to these social changes. However, the restaurant is not merely a convenience spawned by economic and industrial changes; it is also a site of psychological formation, an instrument in the long history of cultural change in which new manners, customs, desires and lifestyles have been cultivated.

While we must eat regularly to survive physically, how we do so makes eating a culturally significant matter. The pursuit of consumer pleasures en masse distinguishes the contemporary West. In the nineteenth century, Thorstein Veblen (1899) referred to this conduct as conspicuous consumption and described it as a new, self-propelling impulse. Individuals did not consume on the basis of identifiable needs, but rather to demonstrate their capacity to consume. Consumption was not limited by need, but was unleashed by the imagination and the desire for novelty. Individuals learned to use commodities to define and enhance themselves, to become more visible and admirable to others.

Dining out puts our sensibilities on display. A restaurant's decor and ambience add to the mood and sensory presence; for instance, with the style of furniture. A tapestry-covered chair suggests wealth in ways that a wooden or plastic chair does not, and similarly the stiffness and whiteness of the napery, whether the tablecloth is cotton, damask or paper, the added table decoration of a single stem flower or Italian candlestick – all these express aesthetic values and become components of an enunciated style. The decor and the menu map onto our expectations of pleasure and amusement; they are instruments for eliciting certain sensations. The plush leather upholstery, dim lighting, huge wall paintings in bright colors, carpeted floors or bare boards strewn with peanut shells as in the rustic pub – all these activate certain moods and emotions that may range from casual fun to social superiority. In both a literal and figurative sense, the restaurant is an instrument bringing certain emotions to the surface. It is a highly engineered environment that conceals its underpinnings. The diner is attracted by excitement and anticipation. A sense of romance can be aroused in a bistro that is atmospheric and exclusive; small tables that bring diners into close proximity but are well spaced from others contribute to a sense of intimacy. High ceilings, soft music – some light Handel, slow Mozart, cool Brubeck – enhance the mood. Similarly, a sense of frivolity is easily manufactured in a parodic café where a fake atmosphere of a bygone or fanciful era has been re-created through the furnishings and the costuming of the waiters, who may be kitted out in sailor suits, geisha gowns or cowboy chaps. The theatricality of the restaurant is integral to its promise to entertain.

When the close-up film shot was introduced in cinema in the 1930s, it brought the full human face of the actor, a stranger, into intimate focus. The details of the eyes, lips and gaze became palpably close. This proximity was like the intimacy found in the physical closeness between lovers and between parents and babies, but rarely if ever before experienced between strangers. This cinematic innovation marked a moment when audience reactions were forced to confront a new subjective experience. The close-up revealed that the slight twist of the lips, the suggestion of a smile, the merest glint in the eye represented certain psychological properties. Motive, desire, fear, anxiety, love and hate were written into these details. The nuances of facial expression were understood to be the signs of another's subjectivity. With the innovations of cinematic technology, a great swathe of individuals was trained en masse to read subjectivity from such details. In the cinema, and then beyond, a confrontation with subjectivity became unavoidable. Not only did the close-up provide a study of the stranger's expression, it also offered a means to penetrate their thoughts; and this in turn transformed psychology into entertainment.

In parallel, the restaurant has similarly been a device that has generated new ways of looking and feeling. It is in the restaurant that we have learned to experiment and adopt certain postures and rehearse social disguises. The restaurant operates as more than a dispenser of food and drink; it also caters to the demand for emotional pleasure and continuous entertainment. It is part of the fashion industries that promulgate taste. It is a showcase for an array of luxuries that have become the expected standards of living in contemporary society, and as such has come to occupy a central place across two centuries of the modern consumer revolution.

Party to the shaping of emotions, the restaurant supplies an inventory of valued subjectivities. Romance, community, urbanity, cosmopolitanism, exuberance and playfulness can all be found in the particular choice of restaurant. Fashion too plays a role, as waves of eating styles emerge and then subside: country-style, provincial, minimal, postmodern, baroque splendor and global restaurants have all found a place in the public domain, as have styles of cuisine such as Asian, fusion, nouvelle, British modern, traditional French, Mediterranean, Italian, fresh, organic and vegetarian. The variety in restaurants industrializes the dining experience by making it a manufactured pleasure. In some instances, these engineered environments fail to work and can be undercut by misreading the fashions. Drinking wine can be difficult and less pleasurable if served in awkwardly shaped, outsized but voguish glasses; eating from an octagonal platter favored by the early adopters of nouvelle cuisine can be irritating when the table top is too small. The sudden collapse of nouvelle cuisine can be partly related to its modishness; in this instance, the expectation of comfort and satisfaction attached to dining out was not provided in plentiful enough supply.

To understand the popularity of dining out, it is necessary to explore how modern social habits and manners have been formed. How we conduct ourselves in public and wish to be seen by others influences the value we place on certain kinds of activities. The café we choose for breakfast, Starbucks or Brunetti's; the lunch we prefer, a sandwich from the local deli or a McDonald's cheese-burger; and who we eat with, at what time of day or night, bring attention to our personal tastes and appetites. The demeanor of the waiter too has altered radically over time. In the early twentieth-century restaurant, they could be intimidating and alarming for the unpracticed diner, but the contemporary food server (so renamed) at Hooters, for instance, is now the butt of urban jokes, while the waiter at the new African restaurant specializing in Nguni beef is a knowledgeable resource who explains the benefits of the different cuts.

These seemingly ordinary, even trivial, practices are part of the emotional economy in which we pursue our pleasures and comforts. While restaurants vary a great deal in style and menu, cost and histories, they are alike insofar as they locate us in the public domain where our predilections are put on display to be observed by others. The restaurant can appear to be a convenience, where we choose to celebrate special occasions, or where we hope to find a new taste sensation. They enable us to enjoy an evening of high expectations as well as being a risky place where these hopes can be ruined by an insouciant waiter or noisy neighboring diner. It is a setting where we are emotionally exposed in the public pursuit of our private interests. While the restaurant is ostensibly about the culinary arts, it is also an instrument that brings focus to our emotional experiences and defines popular practices in the art of everyday living. It is this aspect of dining out that is the pastime's most remarkable but often its most obscure feature.

Early writing about food, from Elizabeth David, Waverley Root and Julia Child, focused on styles of cooking and innovative tastes to educate readers and develop their palate; more recent reportage focuses on the display of the restaurant, its reputation and the experience it offers. There is a contrast in the quality of the writing by Elizabeth David, say, and that of the metro magazine journalists, even though all appear intent on educating the reader. Alongside such popular writing, there are scholarly investigations that concentrate on the logistics of global food production (Nestle 2002; Clapp 2012) and the ethics of consumption (Foer 2009). The anthropology of food is another area of writing that has developed over the past century and continues to examine the functionality of food as a constituent of a viable culture. With the globalized economy strengthening throughout the late twentieth century, the economies of food have assumed greater prominence. Clapp reports on the massive food business now reaching global retail sales of $8 trillion annually and the concentration of wealth with three companies – Wal-Mart, Carrefour and Tesco (Clapp 2012: 109–10). Lang and Heasman (2004: 206) report that the advertising spend by the large food corporations exceeds $40 billion per year, which is greater than the GDP of more than half the world's nations.

The questions explored in this book revolve around the popularity of the restaurant – not only as a place where gastronomic tastes and innovations in food presentation and style are displayed, but as a public stage for self-display and a laboratory in social experimentation. These changes in attitude reflect broader social values about food itself, as well as changes in the pursuit of pleasure and the cultivation of appetites as elements in the fashioning of modern identity. With these considerations in mind, a closer look at the inside operations of the restaurant can be considered a means for examining the formation of elements of subjectivity, and how much this may be primed by the entertainment industries in which the restaurant itself is firmly embedded.

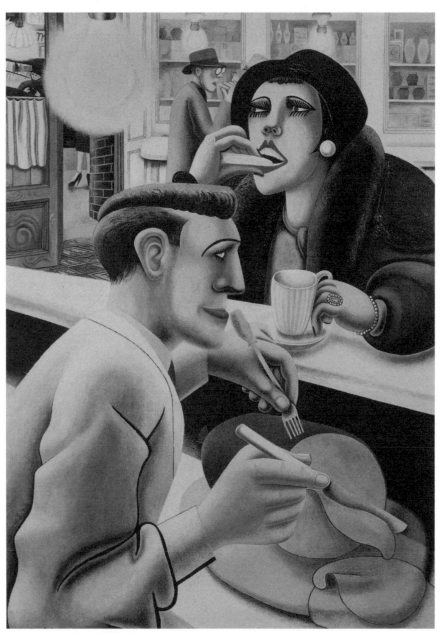

The Snack Bar, 1930 by Edward Burra, Oil on canvas
© Tate, London 2011

1 FASHIONABLE FOOD

The painting of *The Snack Bar* by Edward Burra illustrates the *blasé* attitude that Georg Simmel (1905) identified as the key requirement for a successful life in the crowded noisy city of the industrialized West. The woman eating at the bar is staring into the middle distance. She is unaccompanied, a solo diner, having a quick snack. She has not removed her coat or hat so is not preparing to make herself comfortable enough for a long stay. She appears oblivious to the man working behind the bar as he, in turn, is inattentive to her. Neither seems unduly discomforted by their close physical proximity; indeed, both are depicted as enjoying a sense of privacy, of self-enclosure, while still being aware of strangers close by. The painting could be a snapshot of any lunch or coffee bar almost anywhere in the urban West. It represents an everyday event – solo diners, eating and drinking while reading the newspapers, texting on a mobile phone or gazing into space. Burra's painting is ethnographic; it describes the ordinary as well as raising questions about it, implicitly inviting commentary. The industry of the worker behind the bar slicing meat is juxtaposed with the upturned face of the diner with her unfocused gaze. The picture captures the anomic social values of the advanced metropolis; people in close physical proximity but socially distanced.

Dining out, like other contemporary leisure activities, brings together the consumer ethic and the importance invested in commodities with our personal values. Being fashionable with appearance, with the places we vacation, with types of sporting activities and the leisure habits we cultivate, are all practices that illustrate how much of our everyday life is shaped by market trends (Illouz 1997). The restaurant is part of that engineering process in which personal desires find a visible expression. Regarding food as part of our self-presentation makes it an element in our emotional repertoire. In 1825, when Jean-Anthelme Brillat-Savarin quipped 'we are what we eat', he may well have been alluding to these intricate and complex connections.

The location of the private in the public is part of emotional capitalism and part of the connection between everyday practices within the modern economy. Early nineteenth-century Paris has been described as having a restaurant on every corner, providing for every conceivable taste. These bustling eating and drinking establishments shaped the character of the modern city not only by creating crowds of strangers who came from various social strata and joined in an unregulated mix, but also as social barometers that sensitively recorded political influences and social undercurrents. Spang (2000: 172) noted that the individuals who used the restaurant were making history, they were the new cosmopolitans: "to be conversant with the protocols, rituals, and vocabulary of restaurant going was to be quintessentially Parisian and supremely sophisticated". The restaurant has been and continues to be part of a profound shifting of conventions and customs in which individual sensibilities are cultivated and then compressed into certain requirements of social life. The standards of civility and conformity expected in the public domain become part of the protocols of the restaurant. We learn to be cosmopolitan and sophisticated within its concentrated physical space.

Eating is self-evidently a sensory pleasure and essential for survival, but it is transformed when it takes place in a restaurant. Dining out shifts eating beyond the physiological into the realms of the cultural and economic; hence the opportunity arises to view the restaurant as a vehicle for the pursuit of various interests. The restaurant is not only dedicated to the culinary arts; it is also an arena that effectively introduces and cultivates appetites and desires; it encourages experimentation with food as well as sociality. It is less a dispensary of comestibles and more a stage upon which we stumble about looking for different forms of satisfaction.

Much of the pleasure of dining out can be ascribed to the cultivation of privacy, and most particularly to the atomized delights of being alone in a crowd: of enjoying a sense of distance from the proximity of others while also being entertained by their antics. However, finding pleasure in the public in these circumstances requires a distinctive mentality; in particular, it requires a balancing of the tensions of being self-aware and self-regulating while seeking out and satisfying private desires under the watchful and sometimes censorious gaze of strangers.

Food has a rich intellectual and social history. It has been transformed from a coarse, natural need into a sublimated and aesthetic pleasure and, in some elite circles, a symbol of esoteric knowledge. Braudel (1979: 190) has described the vulgarity of early eating styles with the example of the fourteenth-century banquets of the French aristocracy, where massive platters of meat were served in pyramids mixed with fish and vegetables. This gluttonous style was not limited to the upper class but, referring to Montaigne's description of food styles common to the fifteenth and sixteenth centuries, Braudel reports that the convention was for meat of various kinds to be served in heaped quantities.

Included in this mountain of meat was a range of game as well as beef, mutton, pork, goat, lamb, partridges, waterfowl, larks and flamingos. The sixteenth-century painting by Paolo Veronese, *The Wedding at Cana* (Louvre, Paris), gives some indication of the luxury of these banquets. It shows more than a hundred guests at the table eating delicacies offered at the end of a sumptuous meal.

Food habits are commonly thought of as signs of the individual's social status and culture. The broadest division has traditionally been between those groups who consumed vegetables and those who ate meat and, as a corollary, the former were locked into land cultivation and thus were more placid, while the latter were continuously hunting for their food and were characterized as more aggressive and marauding. Braudel (1979: 104–265) has provided a detailed analysis of crop growing throughout Europe and Asia in the pre-modern period, and maps the changes in social structure that emerge as diets and food sources alter with increased variety in foodstuffs and the greater consumption of meat.

Changing diet transforms everyday lives and societies. This is recognized in the adoption of new habits such as the consumption of tobacco, potatoes, maize and tomatoes. With each new experience there were accompanying social permutations. Most obviously trade and markets became more familiar, stable features in local areas; they introduced new foods and were as well the source of more varied sociability between traders and customers. At different times of the year, markets would trade in plentiful commodities such as game in October, wood and hay in November, grain in December and so on (Braudel 1979: 140–1).

Food has been regulated in all societies by explicit rules about what can and cannot be eaten and by whom and in which particular circumstance. Food preferences and habits report on the individual's status. Food itself is categorized along a continuum from common and ordinary staples to the rare, costly and exotic. Thus it is a social marker. Tastes in food illuminate personal habits as much as do patterns of consumption. Food is central to the symbolic structure of society and fundamental to every economy. As such, it is part of the rituals of reciprocity and obligation that display individual status, wealth and power. In the industrialized society, food has been radically transformed into a commodity that is a commercial powerhouse underpinning much of the globalized trade that has built the economies of the West. Indeed, it was the trade in spices that helped to create the respective empires of the Dutch, English and French. During the fifteenth century, pepper was so highly prized it was known as black gold and valued as much.

Given its centrality in the history of social development, food readily becomes a representation of something else. It is like a fulcrum that balances various attitudes, and the restaurant works in much the same way to refigure food as expressive of diverse interests; as such, it is simultaneously a spectacle, entertainment, convenience and a site for commodity exchange. In this way, food plays a part in framing our modern mentality. By tracing its migratory path between the mouth and the mind, the coarse and refined, the natural and aesthetic, food outlines a silhouette of the contemporary social subject, of how we think of ourselves as discerning, knowing cosmopolitans.

When we choose then to dine out, we are immediately inserted into a complex universe of meanings that stretch from the local to the global, from the historic to the contemporary. The entertainment we derive from dining out hinges on an intricate interplay between the global processes of commodification and the discourses of fashion as it plays into our subjective formulations. When we choose to eat at McDonald's rather than KFC, we are automatically speaking to others, although the content of that message is almost impossible to comprehend. We might be saying we approve of the global trade agreements that have ensured we can purchase a relatively inexpensive meal that is quality controlled so well that we can rely on the same hamburger being available in Tulsa or Tokyo. Alternatively, we might be suggesting that flavor alone and not the economic and political background of food retail has determined our choice. Either way, eating the hamburger delivers cultural messages about fast food, the politics of agribusiness and global food distribution, as well as messages about our personal tastes.

We cannot repeatedly dine in celebrated restaurants that promise specialized menus and dazzling decor, and convincingly claim that our pleasure is only in the food. Nor can we habitually eat at a fast food restaurant and account for the enjoyment by pointing to the speed of the service. In these instances, the cultural meanings of these respective restaurants illustrate the pleasures we are seeking. An obvious attraction of eating in a restaurant is that we are likely to be observed. We have not elevated other physiological needs, say, for sleep, sex or excretion to this level of public visibility. In the restaurant, we are highly visible, and if we are to enjoy our private pleasures in this exposed environment we must cultivate certain sensibilities suited to the circumstances. In this way, the restaurant has the double purpose of being an architecture of public desire as well as an inventory of private sensations. It supplies a vocabulary for shaping emotion and appetites that extend beyond the edible.

DEFINING THE RESTAURANT

The idea of the restaurant as a place of nourishment has numerous antecedents: it is linked to the cook shops in the medieval city that prepared foods for those without servants and home kitchens, which included most people in the lower social orders; it is associated with the seventeenth-century coffee houses that arose in London as purveyors of coffee and tobacco, and as vibrant meeting places for the exchange of information about goings-on in the city, Parliament, at the docks and markets. In various parts of Europe and Asia, elements of the modern restaurant are found in bazaars, travelers' inns and village kitchens. All these are rudimentary restaurants insofar as they meet the appetitive needs of paying custom-ers. However, it is not only this capacity to provide food that characterizes the modern restaurant as much as the influence the restaurant has exerted on social values. The opportunities provided by the restaurant for its patrons to mix with a wide range of people, to disport oneself in public in the guises of invented characters enacted at will, to posture and pretend and to participate in the spread of news and views, has made the restaurant a welcome site in shaping the variety of personal pleasures available within contemporary cosmopolitan life.

Defining the restaurant is not simple as its origins can be traced out in various directions. If we emphasize the culinary, the restaurant can be defined through its menu and style of cooking, and the provision of food becomes its single defining factor. Mennell (1985: 134–44) has described the existence of this kind of rudimentary restau-rant as having existed for centuries before the emergence of its recognizably modern form. The French revolution of the late eighteenth century is cited as the catalyst for the restaurant, by creating a professional class of highly skilled cooks who no longer served an aristocratic household and who found a new form of living by opening public eating places; yet the practice of selling food in the public arena pre-dates this by several centuries. Travelers' inns are an instance where a set meal was available at a price. Food was prepared by a cook and the customer received whatever was the fare of the day. As such, restaurants or similar operations existed in the medieval cities of the twelfth century where cook shops provided hot dishes mainly to those in the lower social ranks who did not have kitchens or cooks available to them.

The choice of food and style of its presentation are also defining features of the restaurant. Mennell (1985: 137) describes the English tavern as capable of providing exclusive dining to a small gathering of socially superior gentlemen as well as catering for vast banquets of a thousand or more diners who might be brought together by local dignitaries in a show of their civic power. In these instances, the tavern functioned in much the same way as a modern restaurant. In different countries and regions, the evolution of the restaurant has taken different pathways, largely determined by local factors. For instance, in France, the practice of selling certain quantities and cuts of meat was controlled by a guild of *traiteurs* during the eighteenth century, which meant that providing small dishes to single customers, as might be required in a restaurant or inn rather than to large households, did not really develop. Meanwhile in England, in contrast, there was less control over the trade of food, thus allowing a catering cadre to develop which served anyone who could afford to purchase the product. During the decades of social upheaval of the French revolution, the influx of provincial deputies into Paris brought new rustic dishes into the city that in time expanded the repertoire of Parisian restaurants, servicing the growing numbers of urban dwellers (Mennell 1985: 139). The selling of particular dishes or specialties marked a further development in the restaurant which again largely pre-dated the French revolution, even though those events did propel the social and economic conditions underlying the marketing of food and style. In England, the existence of a functional Parliament in the seventeenth century created a local economy in which a variety of services were developed for its members and functionaries, including the procurement of meals at all times of the day and night.

The restaurant changed cultural practices around food and continues to be highly effective in shaping individual tastes. The French word *restaurant* originally referred to a restorative or health-giving bouillon or consommé, often heavily reduced and thickened into a paste. It describes a specifically French fashion to imbibe a medicinal juice as a restorative for sickly individuals (Furetière, *Dictionnaire Universel*, 1708). From about the fifteenth to the eighteenth centuries, the semi-medicinal *restaurant* informed the medico-culinary discourses, especially of the Parisian upper classes. The widespread concern with body processes, especially with digestion, circulation of the blood and respiration, meant that individuals of "taste" often suffered from headaches, "nerves" and weaknesses of the chest and stomach, and they frequently needed the health-giving powers of a restorative. It was *de rigueur* for the aristocrat to seek out the best *restaurants* and quietly imbibe them as a solitary act of self-improvement. As the dissipated aristocrat sought the health-restoring elixir from the local *restaurateur,* an important liaison was being established that connected the personal with the commercial and, more specifically in this case, private vice with public prosperity. Thus the indulgences of the upper classes were seen as commercial opportunities for a growing class of merchants. The new habit of enjoying a *restaurant* marked out the identity of its consumers who were at first the dissipated aristocracy and then, as fashions for the habit circulated, the new gentry. The practice was so closely associated with social status that when a parvenu or fop used a *restaurant* to disport himself, it was obvious he was social climbing and not cultivating his good health (Spang 2000: 37–9).

The transformation of the term from its original meaning as an ingredient of a fashionable health regime to a public place to eat and drink follows the modernizing trajectory of the past two centuries. In Paris, in 1782, a take-out shopkeeper named Beauvilliers is credited with establishing the first in-principle modern restaurant. He did so by including in his shop, La Grande Taverne de Londres, a number of small tables and chairs to serve seated customers with a variety of cooked dishes. By serving on the premises, Beauvilliers is credited with the original concept (Mennell 1985: 139). A restaurant was now being referred to as a place where meals could be purchased at various times of the day and night. Rebecca Spang has argued that the concern with food, nutrition, diet and health was a commonplace interest in intellectual and aristocratic circles of the time, and the emergence of the restaurant was, as a result, a predictable outcome. She identifies Mathurin Roze de Chantoiseau as the inventor of the modern restaurant. He promulgated ideas about the merchandizing of comestibles, and notably produced an *Almanach* in 1769 that alphabetically listed thousands of Parisian merchants and businesses in an effort to direct visitors to the city to the available goods and services (Spang 2000: 12–20). In this exercise, he was demonstrating an astute knowledge of marketing principles by promoting food and novelty as the latest fashions. He understood that the desire to consume was also a search for fashionability and personal distinctiveness. Thus, his creation of the restaurant was integral to the growth of urban commerce.

These originary moments, however, cannot be singled out from other preceding circumstances. Two decades earlier, in Paris, a soup vendor named Boulanger provided a place for the consumption of his restoratives, and in the 1760s, in New York, Samuel Fraunces opened a public house in lower Manhattan (not yet so named) where he sold beer and food, and hence could be regarded as a restaurateur. In the previous century in London, in the 1660s, coffee houses were popular and these too can be seen as forerunners of the modern restaurant.

The singular feature of the modern restaurant that links its past and present is the opportunity it gave to individuals to enter the excitement of the social sphere at any time of the day or night, without requiring formal membership or invitation. Mennell (1985: 141) downplays this aspect of the restaurant even as he refers to Samuel Johnson's eighteenth-century observation that dining out provided relief from the anxieties of entertaining guests at home. A host must always be alert to the mood of his guests, but when dining out in a restaurant, there is no such anxiety; instead, there is much greater opportunity to encounter the unexpected. Thus, it is recognized that a great attraction of the restaurant is the possibility it provides for the occurrence of unanticipated pleasures. The modern restaurant becomes an emotional space in which new sensations and states of mind can be discovered and enjoyed. In a recent memoir of Europe at the turn of the twentieth century, the café is described as a haven for young men hungry for news of the world and companionship that brought intellectual excitement. The café was territorialized so that each could have his own table where his particular interests were on view, whether it was the newspaper or tomes of higher learning (de Waal 2010: 128):

> *Every young man has his own Cafe, and each is subtly different.... . You could spend your whole day here, nursing a single cup of coffee under the high vaulted ceilings, writing, not-writing, reading the morning newspaper ... while waiting for the afternoon edition.... . Even the waiters were rumoured to join in the conversations around the huge circular tables. It was, in a memorable phrase of the satirist Karl Kraus, 'an experimental station for the end of the world'. In a cafe you could adopt an attitude of melancholic separation. This was an attitude shared by many ... the most one could be expected to do was talk.*

TOYING WITH FOOD

Non-edible food has also played a part in establishing the importance of the restaurant. An early sixteenth-century treatise, *Work on the Art of Cooking* produced by Bartolomeo Scappi (c.1550–1577), described lavish banquets where architectural feats were achieved using various foods that were not to be consumed. Such virtuoso practices endured in some quarters into the nineteenth century, when celebrity chefs such as Antonin Câreme (1784–1833) designed pastry dishes of equal extravagance. His *Grande Cuisine* appropriated landscape architecture and the organic forms of nature, transforming them into inedible ornaments such as small-scale pagodas, pavilions, rotundas, fountains, thatched cottages, country homes, fortresses and temples, crafted from sugar and wax and sometimes standing four and five feet high. These *pièces montées* with Italian, Turkish, Russian, Chinese, Egyptian and Gallic themes were positioned in the center of a large restaurant table where they were to be looked upon with wonder but not consumed. Food was treated as a material with a strong visual component that could stimulate the palate without necessarily becoming the ingestible. Câreme's inventions were designed, with some deliberation, to distract the diner from the quality of the food that was offered at the dining table. As the forerunner for the table centerpiece, these food-toys make today's single flower stem or decorative candle seem rather paltry. The shifting conventions around the presentation of food make it an object of fashion: in 2010, Lady Gaga made global news with her meat outfit – a hat, clutch bag and clinging dress made from a pink and white marbled material that suggested raw beef (http://www.bbc.co.uk/news/magazine-11297832).

The elaborate *pièces montées* of the nineteenth-century food sculptures herald the twentieth-century examples produced by the Dadaists and Riyochi Majima's studio, Majimart, where body parts are sculpted from food and then shrink-wrapped and packaged as if they were to be marketed in the display refrigerators found in the ubiquitous high street supermarket. More recently, there are entertaining fashions in cake shapes for weddings, birthday and celebratory occasions that are created to reflect the customer's interests and hobbies; for instance, a football stadium, high-heeled shoes, the domestic pet, house and garden, or a glamorous motor car.

Architectural food with its wondrous engineering is extravagant, impressive and amusing and, at the same time, it comments on general attitudes towards the status and role of food in affluent societies. The visual properties of food are being elevated above the nutritional. Nouvelle and haute cuisine are being likened to an art form and, like a painting that shows a horse or dog or human face in a new way, never thought of before, so too does elaborate cuisine change our perceptions. The Dadaists toyed with food, making it a material for lampooning the prosaic middle classes. In the 1950s, Barry Humphries, the alter ego of Dame Edna Everage, used various kinds of baked cake (lamingtons, fruitcake, sponge fingers, rainbow tiara cake, Swiss roll) to create multi-colored and textured landscape paintings that mocked the popularity of the decorative landscape painting found on the walls of middle class homes of the new suburbs.

Architectural food continues to comment on our physical and aesthetic appetites. The contemporary Japanese artist, Ryoichi Majima, has used food sculptures to highlight the growing power of food manufacturers and retailers. In 1995, he exhibited two large sculptures, *Noodle Boy* and *Noodle Girl,* that decry the alarming future of global food production. Each piece consisted of a round ceramic rice bowl, common to many Asian restaurants, but executed to stand about six feet in diameter. *Noodle Boy* has a fashionable Mohawk haircut of the time and on his face, a wide-eyed, open expression. Majima has immersed him in a bowl with only his head and shoulders visible above a soup containing large pieces of floating spring onion, bamboo shoots, water chestnut, bacon and noodles. The tendons in his neck are strained as his mouth is forced wide open while being stuffed with long strands of noodle entwined about two gigantic, suspended chopsticks. The complementary *Noodle Girl* also sits in a large bowl filled with soup and floating vegetable matter. Like *Noodle Boy*, her head is tilted back and her mouth is gagging on food forced down her throat from over-arching chopsticks. Majima is commenting on the epicurism that dominates the global food market and the consequences of our tastes for fashionable and gourmet pleasures. He depicts the consumer (*Noodle Boy/Girl*) as being over-fed and dominated by external and invisible forces; perhaps the remote agribusinesses that determine types of crop production and patterns of global food distribution (see http://www.banquete.org/exposicionIngles/majimaIngles/majima.htm).

Again, using food for political reasons is not new. The beginning of still life painting in the late sixteenth century marked a shift into a new era of concern with the solemnity of food as an economic commodity and product of materialism. The vivid realism of still life paintings emphasized the difficulty of dividing the real from the representational. The depiction of grapes, vegetables and flowers by Felipe Ramirez (1628, Prado, Madrid) and two fruit bowls by Tomas Hiepes (1642, Prado, Madrid) mark a moment when ordinary household objects were re-valued as symbols of high culture. Such paintings of food celebrate economic growth: in the next century, Luis Meléndez (1770) painted the chocolate service as a homage to the success of Spanish traders bringing chocolate to Europe.

Both the trend for playing with food as sculptural material and the transformation of food into a symbol of economic and political prosperity have long histories that still reverberate through our contemporary customs. Table settings described by Montaigne in 1580 resemble our current practices with the use of crockery, tablecloths, napkins, lighted candles and small dishes of salt or olive oil. The sixteenth century marks a moment when individual spoons and knives were provided by the host of the meal rather than individuals bringing their own implements. Individual settings included a plate, cup, spoon and knife and sometimes a fork, but these elements took varying amounts of time to become customary. Previously, there were shared cups and plates and individuals used their hands to select morsels from a common bowl or platter.

Individual forks were among the last of the modern implements to find their way to the table. These changes slowly altered the rules in which individuals shared physical space and practices (Braudel 1979: 203–6).

These changes reflect the influences that fashion our appetites and reveal an increasing concern with the sensibilities of others. Inserting one's hands into a common bowl to select food, drinking from a collective cup shared by others, discarding unwanted morsels by returning them to common vessels were becoming increasingly unacceptable practices. This is indicative of a growing self-consciousness about manners and public behavior, and it is the dining table that becomes the focus for these cultural innovations. The act of being in physical proximity with others is the catalyst for increasing thresholds of tolerance, as Norbert Elias (1978) has described. People learned to observe others more closely, to react to their habits and to increasingly influence one another to be less offensive, more tolerant, and more aware of the impact of one's bodily functions on the comfort of others. These same concerns occur in the modern restaurant where the regulation of privacy in public has shaped the protocols of dining out. Toying with food by making it work as art or part of an elaborate table setting that ritualizes the presentation and consumption of food gives emphasis to the cultural value it universally attracts. In the specificities of the rituals and playfulness are indications of food's social and political status. In an age of abundance, too much food produces excessive waste that can be measured in terms of the amount of time dedicated to food preparation, as in nouvelle cuisine, or in the elaborate packaging that accompanies snack and fast foods. Attitudes to food as art, as entertainment, as status symbol and so on are indications of some of the cultural values that pattern everyday living.

FOOD RULES

Every society, irrespective of its economic organization as agrarian, feudal, capitalist or communal, has surrounded food with a symbolic system that transforms it into cultural rules. These in turn demonstrate status as well as more ephemeral qualities such as individual elan and sangfroid. Marcel Proust begins 4,000 pages of *Remembrance of Things Past* with the memory of madeleines. Food is associative; bread and wine have become flesh and blood in the sacrament. The color, texture and shape of food, the place where it is purchased, who has prepared it and where it is consumed all influence its social significance and meaning.

To see the restaurant as a machine producing distinctive social habits focuses attention on the changing social value and representation of food. In recent years, various cooking programs have appeared on television, the role of chef has been given celebrity status, millions of recipe books have been published, and serious film documentaries of regional culinary histories have been made, as well as investigative exposés on the workings of the mass production food industries. Food has become newsworthy, perhaps even more so since the events of large-scale animal herd disease and global food contaminations (BSE, avian flu, horse DNA in processed meats). The rise of the supermarket as a powerful financial corporation (Wal-Mart) with increasingly sophisticated marketing techniques has radically heightened public awareness of food quality as a means of promoting the highly packaged, quality-controlled products it dispenses. Health issues such as BMI monitoring and national levels of obesity have also reinforced the view of food as an item on the social and political agenda.

Food is a social signifier and as such it is both empty and over-determined. It can be a credential and proof of identity – Jews, Hindus, Catholics, men, women, infants, the aged all eat differently, and as such have aspects of their identities attached to how they eat. Food also indicates more febrile states such as mood or mental disposition; fasting can be a sign of religiosity (starving for atonement or penance) or renunciation as in dieting, and bingeing a sign of distraction and mental disorder. Food produces an ever-expanding social language, and this has been speeded up by the processes of industrialization that keep changing its appearance, ensuring its plasticity and making it "endlessly interpretable, as gift, threat, poison, recompense, barter, seduction, solidarity, suffocation" (Eagleton 1998: 204).

Consuming food has a decorative value according to Roland Barthes (1972: 59); it speaks of other qualities. How and when we eat and drink embeds us in associative circumstances – so drinking wine in cold weather reminds us of warmth; drinking wine in the heat of summer evokes "all things cool and sparkling". The preparation of red meat differs according to class; it is served flat "like the sole of a shoe in cheap restaurants" and "thick and juicy" in the bistros favored by the middle classes, while the upper classes prefer it "moist throughout beneath a light charred crust, in haute cuisine". Steak is for Barthes a sign of patriotic values, and the *frites* that accompany it are signs of nostalgia (Barthes 1972: 60–3). He regards food as always associative; it reiterates the class structure and as such is a synecdoche of society.

When we choose to dine out, there is no compulsion to do so; we select a restaurant with an appealing menu and ambience, and in this way we deliberately foreground elements of our emotional repertoire. Our pursuit of pleasure and the display of taste are directed towards others (who may or may not be watching) in a demonstration that we possess certain attributes. To view dining out as a practice that gives shape to personal desires is to see how human emotions can be influenced by circumstance. Dining out is thus a vehicle for highlighting how exchange works with others. It illustrates those moments in which sociability takes on a visible form. The popularity of dining out, however, cannot be explained solely by linking it with an appetite for pleasure – in much the same way that the department store cannot be causally explained as a product of our materialism or the church a direct result of religiosity. The popularity of eating out and its economic significance focuses attention on those everyday habits that have gained widespread importance as elements of a life spent in the densely populated, noisy cities of the modern era. In this sense, eating out is a micro-spectacle of larger social patterns; it reflects new family formations as well as contemporary shifts in desires and how we fashion our social persona. We have been described as taste-based, self-making machines and cultural omnivores who devour our symbolic surrounds in search of identity (Bell and Valentine 1997: 47). Accordingly, as we find pleasure in dining out, the activity itself becomes a beacon that reveals much of the complex exchange between social and economic circumstances and our sense of identity, between what Eva Illouz (2007) has described as the cold intimacies of emotional capitalism and the history of individualism in the West.

A great deal of hyperbole surrounds food. Advertising and the diet industries have emphasized body image and increased concern over health and the moral opprobrium directed at the over-indulged body. The film *Super Size Me* (2004) drew attention to the marketing styles of certain restaurants and the rising trends of obesity in the West. The documentary *Food, Inc.* (2009) looked at the farming and food industries in terms of public health and nutrition.

The set piece in Quentin Tarantino's *Pulp Fiction* (1994), featuring two murderous hit men engaged in a cultural analysis of food by comparing the American cheeseburger and the Parisian Royale, has become a much-referenced iconic moment. Andy Warhol's painted soup cans are almost universally recognizable. The meals served in the popular television series *The Sopranos* generated a cookbook of their recipes. The decade-long popular television sitcom, *Seinfeld*, was partly located in a New York diner. These instances have helped circulate global images of food and restaurants and used the hyperbole associated with both to underscore how food has become both a commercial commodity and site of private fixation.

THE UNIVERSAL MEAL AND THE ORIGINS OF TASTE

Traditionally and cross-culturally, most meals have been constituted from a combination of a starchy core or complex carbohydrate such as rice, wheat or corn, and a protein-giving substance such as meat or legumes – peas, beans or nuts – coupled with a relish or tasty sauce and spice to add interest. Most meals are combinations of these three. Rarely does a meal consist only of one – all starch, all protein, all relish or tidbit. Or at least this was the prevailing custom until the industrialization of food and the growth of the snack food market. The simple three-part combination of starch-protein-relish has been radically altered with the introduction of new food products that provide only one or two of these ingredients. Such changes to diet have introduced portable snack foods that have dislodged the tri-part cooked meal and replaced it with novelties – ice cream is "heaven on a stick"; a sweet cola drink is "the real thing". Food has radically changed appearance and thus become more influenced by fashions and by the entertainment value that this delivers.

While the popularity of snack foods may appear directly connected to changed methods in advertising, other conditions such as agricultural practices and technological advances in food production are also part of the transformation. Fads and fashions in consumer tastes are not linear or causal. The fashionability of tastes is linked to marketing cycles and innovations in manufacture and distribution. Developing tastes for certain products is part of food marketing. Thus the evolution of cooking styles and the manner of food consumption are embedded in social and economic systems. In medieval Europe, for example, the foodstuffs commonly available were meat, fish, game and gruel, and what people ate indicated their social and class ranking. Gruel, a pottage of vegetables, was the daily fare of the lower classes, while game and fish were the staples of the aristocracy and the gentry who rarely if ever ate gruel. The novelty of butchered meat, in its small, portable portions, was the signature of the new merchant class whose members needed to always be ready to move on, perhaps fleeing from a sour transaction or more probably just seeking out new markets (Braudel 1973; Mennell 1985: 41). Diet accurately reflected status and occupation. Its consumption also rested on assumptions about the health of the body and the need to maintain a balance between the cardinal fluids – blood, bile and phlegm. Ideas connecting illness, food and health persisted for centuries and produced a variety of opinions about food values that we would now find quaint. For instance, cabbage was regarded with some trepidation as it produced an increase in black bile, which in turn generated bad dreams and dimmed the vision (Varriano 2009: 12). However, a sense of anxiety attached to food continues into the present, variously attached to concerns over genetically modified grains, the shelf life of food items, packaging information and techniques used in factory production.

In her book, *Italian Food* (1969: 169), the celebrated Elizabeth David describes in rich detail how the early morning light in Venice makes the food stalls in the market into a visually exciting and subtle panorama: "here the cabbages are cobalt blue ... the colors of the peaches, cherries and apricots ... are reflected in the rose-red mullet". Paintings during the Renaissance frequently depicted foods in varying degrees of naturalism. Caravaggio's *Basket of Fruit*, thought to be painted between 1596 and 1598, and thus one of the earliest paintings of an everyday banal topic, depicts ripe fruit heaped into a woven basket. The naturalism of the apples, grapes, figs and leaves, with the hint of imperfection and blemish, makes the subject appetizing as if it begs to be eaten. Other depictions of food represent it within a more religious setting; as part of the sacred it is simpler and more ascetic, such as a round of bread and chalice of wine. As still life painting took on a vivid and naturalistic appearance, a more modern attitude to food began to emerge. For instance, a sixteenth-century guidebook to various Italian pleasures provides a list of foods that would be familiar to a shopper of the twenty-first century; it recommends Cremona for the best beans, Comacchio for salted eels, Ferrara for prosciutto, Piacenza for cheese and Parma for melons (Varriano 2009: 39), as we might recommend Italian olive oil, unpasteurized French cheese and Israeli dates.

Elizabeth David (1969 14) has pointed out that provincial dishes are rightly celebrated for their unique qualities which include their seasonality. In reality, provincial cooking is always seasonal: the bouillabaisse of Provence, the cassoulet of the Languedoc, and the coq au vin of Burgundy are not prepared every day by local restaurateurs but only when the produce is available or for special occasions. However, this quality has been largely lost to commercialism; the number of customers who are seeking authentic provincial dishes has escalated since the mid-twentieth century. The demand for authentic cuisine exceeds the availability of the actual ingredients of the dishes. As a result, opportunistic restaurateurs lure gullible new customers with the promise of authentic and fashionable cuisine. It is David's contention that the rise in popularity of the road-side convenient café – in some ways, the forerunner of the global chain restaurant – played a crucial part in ensuring the inauthenticity of regional cuisine by catering to the demands of the tourist diner, in and out of season.

Against a background where changes are evolving across numerous social spheres, a definitive history of gastronomy and the culinary arts is difficult, even fruitless, to attempt. It is impossible to identify the points of change when less spiced dishes gave way to more natural flavors, or when mannered appearances – say, the crafting of fish to resemble a goat's head or the presentation of a counterfeit ham made of salmon and gelatin – were replaced with a desire for authentic flavors and textures. Norbert Elias (1982: 232), in his history of the civilizing process, has suggested that long-term social processes defy accurate dating and certainly the history of gastronomy supports the theory. Culinary history is replete with accounts of the remarkable talents of particular chefs or restaurateurs and how celebrated dishes came into being. There are also narratives of great figures in culinary history who supposedly brought about profound changes such as the introduction of the fork, as with the example of Catherine de Medici who reputedly promoted "those

Italian neatnesses" (Fisher 1954: 75). However, culinary practices tend to appear and disappear and overlap with one another; thus, the fork was used in various shapes and sizes for hundreds of years before it became a convention of the meal table (Braudel 1973: 121ff; Rebora 2001), and styles of medieval cooking practices with the use of heavy spices can be seen to have persisted into the eighteenth century, well after Renaissance cooking conventions had replaced that style (Goody 1982; Revel 1982; Mennell 1985). Infused into this long history of twists and changes in the evolution of eating styles is the importance of table manners, and the growing awareness that others can take offense when we fail to control our behavior and take account of their sensibilities.

FASHIONING APPETITE

The idea that keeps repeating itself in the story of the restaurant is that it harbors novelties and pleasures that promise to satisfy any number of private desires. Its location at the center of the public domain makes it much like the department store in its variety and accessibility. It is instrumental in devising new modes of conduct and feelings as well as compressing the fashions of the day into an apparently limitless range of choices. At the same time, the restaurant itself is a highly regulated operation that conceals its well-worked machinery behind its ambience and reputation. Despite the shifting fashions – *haute cuisine, cuisine classique, bourgeoise, régionale paysanne, terroir, nouvelle* – the restaurant's function remains closely tied to the interests of the consumer economy and emotional capitalism. The intriguing feature of the restaurant that has secured its place in the complex narrative of the emerging modern society is its fashionability, and that, in turn, has made it important as part of the process of re-figuring the balance between the private and public, between vice and virtue, desire and fashion, individual habits and social practices.

In the late seventeenth century, the coffee house emerged in parallel with the changing public spaces of the growing mercantile city. In London, coffee houses began trading from the 1660s, and by 1700 there were hundreds of establishments. They were immediately popular for providing opportunities for association that previously were unlikely. They encouraged the reading of newspapers, conversation about world affairs and the exchange of opinions, and as such they originated new commercial practices and generally provided opportunities for the promiscuous mixing of social ranks and classes. Some conservative reactions to the coffee house depicted it as a hotbed of revolutionary fervor. Nonetheless, its popularity could not be abated. By 1800, there were tens of thousands of such places throughout Europe as well as America. In seventeenth-century Europe, there was an explosion of interest in consumable products, especially coffee, tea and sugar (Mintz 1985). Towards the end of the eighteenth century, the separate diary entries from Samuel Pepys and Samuel Johnson comment on the growing interest in food and drinking as a popular leisure activity, as well as a sign of the growing commercialization of pleasure (Porter 2000: 270).

How we think of the private and public, and what we think is acceptable to do in public, reflects more general views on social propriety. Norbert Elias has argued that increased constraint in the display of manners became more attractive and valued as we became more self-conscious and controlled in our bodily habits. At the dining table, for example, from the history of European manners it became increasingly offensive to gulp food, to eat enormous quantities and spit bits of food onto the floor. To be more constrained and self-conscious changed eating styles and played a part in influencing other associated behaviors such as styles of dress and bodily deportment, conventions in conversation and habits of personal hygiene. By observing such practices, individuals learned to discipline themselves and their appetites. These changes in social practices reflected how we were thinking about others and ourselves. This was particularly evident in the practice of consuming food in public. As we spend more time in close proximity with strangers, we become increasingly self-conscious and aware of our influence on them. Elias states (1982: 274) that a "psychological" view develops from the more precise observations we make of others and ourselves in terms of the longer series of motives and causal connections that we learn are associated with how we are regarded. For instance, as social barriers weaken and greater variety enters everyday life, as we trade with one another and make commercial deals, as we work alongside different classes of people, as families intermarry and children play with one another, then these long-term associations build a capacity for vigilance, for being self-controlled and aware of being continuously observed. Over time, in this new more complicated social environment, we learn to see the importance of how we are regarded and estimated by others. Elias has argued that it is in the exercise of manners, in how we conduct ourselves, that we are provided with critical insights into the workings of society at large.

Elias refers to early accounts of personal deportment to support this view. He draws on the work of Erasmus of Rotterdam and his sixteenth-century treatise on bodily propriety as an early guide to the changes that were taking place in human conduct and how they reflected changes in the character of individual sensibilities towards what we now refer to as the psychological. Erasmus's vivid detailing of personal demeanor such as table manners, alimentation, blowing one's nose, posture and sexual relations are used to indicate how behavior was responding to a growing concern about how others react to such displays (Elias 1978). The ability to see oneself as another might – to exercise a self-reflective imagination – and to practice constraint and discrimination largely because of the awareness of the other's gaze are important influences on human conduct that have taken centuries to evolve into the commonplace manners and social codes that we now employ in everyday life.

As table manners came to be symbolic of social status, it became simultaneously evident that a heightened interest was being paid to one another that included new ways of looking. This attention to gestures and demeanor provided a basis for reading personal traits. The details of the body were being magnified. Fernand Braudel (1973: 137) cites the work of Nicolas de Bonnefons, whose written account of good living (*Les Loisirs des Campagnes*, 1650) was a guide to how and where to eat. Braudel interprets this close attention to habits as indicative of a new emphasis on social styles. He cites Bonnefons on the details of the table setting that included precise measurements on the actual size of the tablecloth and the allocated distance between diners. The purpose of these exact instructions was to enhance the diner's privacy. The tablecloth, it turns out, could be used to cover up the diner's body and the items of clothing that might have been loosened after too great an indulgence of the repast. It could also hide pieces of refused food to avoid the habit of spitting them onto the table or floor. In these detailed descriptions of how to eat, we can see a growing desire to please the other person by not causing offense, and to protect oneself from the other's implied criticism or disdain — especially when encountered across the intimate confines of the dining table.

Food has long been used as a code to control boundaries of inclusion and exclusion, and transactions across social barriers (Douglas 1972: 61). Bourdieu (1984) has identified certain foods as reflective of gender and social status; fish, for example, is more favored by women, and red meat by men. Contemporary practices of food consumption still work as codes. As we develop acuity in observing others, and become hyper-vigilant about the gestures made in the social encounter (eye contact, physical proximity, volume of speech), we simultaneously become more reliant on these cues to interpret complex social maneuvers and displays of power, prestige and position. Thus begins a style of sociality where attention to detail is emphasized.

Personal control in particular becomes associated with prestige; the more reserved and inexpressive we are, the more readily we are regarded as being socially reliable. Being reserved demonstrates a willingness to subsume one's own proclivities and impulses in order to meet the expectations of others. The reserved, obedient and self-controlled individual is much easier to predict and hence is more readily accepted. Such individuals make fewer demands on us. The value and esteem we accord such individuals is a measure of the concern we always have about the fragility of the social situation. The moment in which we engage another is a moment of intense attention as we calculate the temperature of the scene. The estimation of the other's willingness to conform, to follow the standard rules, gives us a sense of how much we may be exposed in whatever follows. A conventional exchange indicates that everyone is willing to observe the rules, and to act as an object to one another. Obedience to the expectations shows an awareness of the situation and how quickly we can disturb others through offensive actions or, conversely, win their favor by acting as they expect. These ideas support the view that in demonstrating personal control, we also enhance our own interests. This makes social status a function of the other's opinion. When we follow the expected repertoire, we are tacitly agreeing to meet the needs of the other. We are demonstrating a willingness to control our own impulses in order to produce a reassuring and predictable situation. In a public place like the restaurant, a great deal rests on the willingness of a collection of strangers to observe the rules and not transgress the tacit thresholds of tolerance. This level of control measures the tension between the private and public realms, between what we might want and what we will do. Historians of manners such as Elias, Braudel and Bourdieu drew on recorded accounts of etiquette to identify these interconnections, and this is still an effective means for understanding how we learn to follow the social rules of everyday conduct today (see also Aries 1962: 406–7; Lévi-Strauss 1978: 507).

THE STATUS OF FOOD

In *Distinction* (1984), an empirical survey of everyday lifestyles, Pierre Bourdieu illustrated the different types of knowledge we possess, and the different social, symbolic, economic and cultural capitals we use. He did this by closely describing the minutiae of ordinary French life; he looked at the kinds of television programs we watched, where we lived and in what kinds of housing; he looked at the spend of discretionary income, what kinds of entertainments we enjoyed, the possessions we valued, the foods we consumed, the jobs we held. By detailing the various lifestyles, Bourdieu gave an account of how differences develop and are maintained in the ways we live. Like Elias and Braudel, Bourdieu also emphasized the importance of food and the customs around eating as indicative of other social features. He described the ordinary meal as an intricate event that transformed the crude reality of bodily sustenance into an instance of complex social display. Food is not only a means of survival; it has aesthetic qualities such as its patterns of color and texture; it has a style of preparation and unique presentation; all of which reflect back on our own self-image (Bourdieu 1984: 196). As he states:

> [T]he manner of presenting and consuming the food, the organisation of the meal and setting of the places, strictly differentiated according to the sequence of dishes and arranged to please the eye, the presentation of the dishes, considered as much in terms of shape and colour (like works of art) as of their consumable substance, the etiquette governing posture and gesture, ways of serving oneself and others, of using the different utensils, the seating plan, strictly but discreetly hierarchical, the censorship of bodily manifestations of the act or pleasure of eating (such as noise or haste), the very refinement of the matter being consumed, with quality more important than quantity – this whole commitment to stylization tends to shift the emphasis from substance and function to form and manner, and so to deny the crudely material reality of the act of eating.

Food is a preoccupation of modern life. Where we eat, with whom, how often, at what cost, and why reveal social practices that reside at the core of culture; understanding how food creates desires and appetites is tantamount to understanding how a society works. From the classic *The Raw and the Cooked* by Claude Lévi-Strauss (1969) to M.F.K. Fisher on *The Art of Eating* (1954), Marion Nestle on *Food Politics* (2002) and Jonathan Safran Foer on *Eating Animals* (2009), an extensive commentary on food and its social importance has been produced. Food is key to understanding the vast array of modern appetites that fuel contemporary society. It is also a fashion item, linked directly with the politics of its production and its global marketing. Food products are continuously being brought to our attention through advertising campaigns, supermarket displays and in food halls and restaurants. Such exposure often illuminates contradictions in our knowledge of food and its production. Our increasing moral outrage at some practices such as battery hen farms and the genetic modification of grains can be at odds with our everyday habits of expecting to satisfy our diverse appetites by sourcing whatever we want in supermarkets and restaurants.

Food and its manner of presentation have become symbols of social differentiation. The changes in styles of eating show that the evolution of the culinary arts cannot be isolated from other changes in human society. Consuming food in public has made us self-conscious, and the restaurant has played an important part in producing the psychological point of view. It is now part of ordinary life that we try to see ourselves as others might, and exercise a psychological imagination in order to practice constraint and discrimination and nullify the intrusiveness of the other's gaze. We have learned to look at each other in new ways and become more attentive to gestures and expressions as signs of other attributes.

Thinking about the semiotics of dining out suggests there is more at stake than just the pursuit of pleasure. It introduces the idea that our sensations are embedded in a much more complex cultural territory from which erupts, every now and again, a suggestion that creates uncertainty about the origins, authority and reliability of our own tastes and pleasures. Dining out may at first appear an ordinary part of daily life, a means by which the body is fuelled, and then life goes on, but its long history and anthropology alerts us to its social magnitude and centrality to human studies. Not only do styles and patterns of eating have long-term economic significance in the industrialized societies of the West, they also place the activity within an emotional grid that supports the consumer values of a highly networked and expanding process of globalization.

The restaurant has played an effective part in defining new sensibilities and appetites. The increasing popularity of dining out has coincided with other cultural innovations that have blurred the boundaries between the private and social. The entertainment and culture industries in particular have dominated the character of the consumer West from the nineteenth century onwards, and they parallel the growth in the fashion for dining out. The transfer of private activities into the public underlies a new appetite for experiencing intimate scenes in public, within close proximity of strangers who may be watching us for their own amusement as we might also in turn be watching them. Thus our private lives have become part of the public spectacle. In a restaurant, we are immediately plunged into an ongoing social stream as if in the midst of a theatrical performance and, at the same time, we can superimpose our own fantasies and desires onto the scene. This manner of acting in the public is important in the wider context of training us to enjoy the particular social appetites that are available in the contemporary world. In this way, the restaurant is instrumental in the construction of the types of personal conduct suitable for life in the specific circumstances of a cosmopolitan consumer society.

Georg Simmel (1905) described these circumstances more than a century ago when he identified the emergence of the metropolis as requiring new social competences and particular sensibilities. As the industrial revolution concentrated economic activities into cities, and as banking, commerce and manufacture produced new modes of employment, individuals came into contact with a much wider variety of people. To survive in the overcrowded, noisy and stimulating city, individuals needed to be both calculating and *blasé*. City dwellers needed to develop a capacity for not being aware of others even as they are physically pressed up against one another, and they needed to possess higher thresholds of tolerance so that any offensive or perturbing displays of cultural difference would not appear to be shocking. This was the *blasé* attitude: to be hyper-aware and simultaneously controlled and expressionless. At the same time, the city provided new opportunities that increased appetites for amusement and novelty. Simmel foresaw that modern city life required a new psychological perspective with heightened thresholds of self-discipline that balanced the conflicting stimulations and demands of intensified social contacts with the need to control the hyper-stimulation that this delivers.

Most changes in human behavior have a tendency to be unsystematic, to bend back upon themselves and persist with contradictions, and the long-term social processes involved in the formulation of the psychological perspective can be considered in this way (Elias 1982: 232). The restaurant has influenced styles of public conduct and defined new pleasures and appetites, and thus has been instrumental in training us to acquire the mental attributes necessary for living in the densely populated cosmopolitan city. The restaurant has been, and continues to be, a liberalizing social invention where experiments in human interaction take place. Norbert Elias (1978: 68) has pointed out that "conduct while eating cannot be isolated. It is a segment – a very characteristic one – of the totality of socially instilled forms of conduct". This suggests that most practices of the everyday can be thought of as reflecting the character of the society at large because they themselves are unmediated reproductions of the status quo. Accordingly, the gestures and manners that we accept as customary elements of daily life carry in them prescribed viewpoints. By connecting public events so closely with the individual's private sensibilities, the idea is being reinforced that "it is the structure of society that demands and generates a specific standard of emotional control" from the individual (Elias 1978: 201). Dining out in this context is a means for shaping interiority. This explains how the artificial and contrived performances required of us in many restaurants cannot be dismissed as merely the demands of circumstances, as if we were forced somehow to be romantic, loud, exuberant, artificial and so on by the nature of the restaurant in which we are dining. These performances are better seen as inseparable from our sense of pleasure; and more, a sense of our own singular identity.

From its modern beginnings, the restaurant linked trade, consumption, contemporary culture and politics. It provided a location in which individuals were free to indulge new desires and experiment with social liaisons. These liberties remain part of its enduring appeal and account in large part for its long-term social success. In many ways, the restaurant is still a site where private interests are re-figured into public prosperity. Its obvious commercial success cannot be separated from the pleasures it provides to millions of individuals which, in turn, suggests that there is a symbiotic closeness between private and public interests. In the early restaurant, people learned how to sit closely alongside strangers without engaging their attention. It was necessary to learn the rules of propinquity. By understanding these basic social principles, we acquired new perspectives. Thus, the restaurant was instrumental in cultivating many of the everyday practices and social appetites associated with modern urban life, particularly the pleasure of purchasing service in a fleeting and calculative transaction from someone who is and most often remains a stranger.

When the mid-twentieth-century commentators on social behavior, Erving Goffman (1961), Peter Berger and Thomas Luckmann (1966), considered the question of how <AQ5> societies and individuals fit together, they worked from the principle that nothing is as it seems, and everything we know must be taught to us in a constantly reiterative manner. Thus everyday rules of sociality needed to be widely repeated so that they came to appear unassailably true. This view has a connection back to early commentaries that argued that when we engage with others, we build up, over time, a repertoire of acceptable behaviors that are calculated to make social life more rewarding. We learn to behave as we are expected, and we subtly adapt our conduct as we interpret the other's reactions to us. This constant exchange of impressions and interpretations means that our knowledge of how society works is largely based on local and idiosyncratic habits and beliefs. It is as if what we know is made sensible and coherent only by reinforcement through repetition and reiteration of what it is that everyone else around us seems to believe.

Thus consuming food in public has made us more self-conscious, and the restaurant has played a part in cultivating the psychological imagination. This perspective has taken centuries to evolve into the taken-for-granted manners and social codes that we now accept as part of ordinary life. How we have learned to look at each other and become more attentive to gestures and expressions as if they were telling signs, and how we have magnified the details of the body and become conscious of the gaze of the other has much to do with the social training tacitly provided in the restaurant and other social arenas in which we now freely associate.

2   TASTE AND DESIRE

He was not experienced at dining in a Western-style restaurant... To his surprise, the black tea came in a tall glass with a Lipton tea bag. The popcorn tasted too sweet and was as tough as rubber. The coffee was fine, but not hot enough... . What surprised him was not the poor quality of the food they were served, but that people were content in spite of it. It seemed as if the atmosphere more than compensated for anything else.

WHEN RED IS BLACK (QIU XIAOLONG)

In the consumer societies of the West, every conceivable idea, practice and material substance has been transformed by market forces into a commodity to be admired and desired, then acquired and possessed. The consumer society puts everything up for sale and food is no exception. The desire for food is not a simple matter of meeting basic nutritional needs; it is part of a complex system through which claims are made for social status and prestige. Food has been transformed into symbol, icon, fashion and tool. It is constantly on display in order to fuel and refresh our appetites. The food items we encounter in fast food outlets, elegant food halls in up-market department stores, on supermarket shelves and exclusive delicatessens and so on have the capacity to speak to us; they are loquacious and often ironic, humored and even deformed in spectacular ways in order to catch our attention. Roland Barthes (1982: 78) has defined food as "a system of communication, a body of images, a protocol of usages, situations and behavior". He is alerting us to food as an object of the times that embodies a spectrum of values that can sometimes appear contradictory. Food is at once a simple necessity and an elegant gesture that reflects the human genius for crafting the environment to meet aesthetic and material interests. Food is the energy in the appetite cycle and must accordingly continue to be amusing, reassuring, esoteric and engaging in order to shape and re-shape our appetites.

The growth of the city and the shift from court to town was integral to immense cultural changes in the early modern period. People became engaged in new social events such as meeting in coffee houses (largely restricted to men), walking the streets and attending expositions and galleries. A more open and liberal public sphere evolved from new modes of public socializing and individuals came to see themselves differently. A heightened sense of anxiety also developed as presenting oneself to an audience of strangers, and anticipating their reactions, made people more conscious of the impressions they made and how identity was apparitional and could be altered at will as well as by accidental disclosure. The popularity of novels, diaries, belles lettres, newspapers and such materials was evidence of a new preoccupation with oneself as a social figure. They also produced a vocabulary for both self-fashioning and taking the measure of others. The popularity of The Life and Opinions of Tristram Shandy (1759–1767) can be considered a turning point when individuals en masse began an infatuation with themselves. There was a growing regard for personal experience, for seeking novelty and adventure, for cultivating feelings and learning about inner truths. Thinking differently about oneself also meant thinking differently about the previously solid precepts of tradition and authority. Thus begins a chronicle of the self as it voyaged inwards to find a core, to identify personal strengths and capabilities. This exploration of the inner realm was largely propelled by contact with the stranger encountered in the teeming and seemingly unregulated society of the expanding city.

In the pre-modern aristocratic world, it was common to serve foods in a manner that concealed their natural origins, and this appeared to coincide with other social changes in human commerce such as more restraint in the performance of courtly manners and the greater exercise of dissemblance. At the same time, quantity was giving way to quality; the huge array of foods of the medieval table, and the great amounts of waste that accompanied it, were being slowly replaced with a concentration on tastier foods. Piquant sauces that highlighted natural flavors rather than overwhelmingly heavy spiced sauces became the norm (Mennell 1985: 72). Individual servings were introduced with separate table settings including bowls, knives and eventually forks for each diner. The courtly fashion in foods was beginning to emphasize the small, delicate and costly, although displays of extravagance were still in evidence in order to demonstrate the wealth and power of the host. For example, a sixteenth-century compendium on the art of cooking described a modest banquet for forty guests as consisting of fifty or more dishes served on 400 pieces of gold and silver tableware with 27 desserts served in 200 dishes. This extravagance was further highlighted with six table decorations of small statues depicting nymphs, exotic creatures and mythological deities created from sugar, butter and pasta. As items of food continued to be used to reflect the aspirations and status of the host, the changing style of presentation and the manner of consumption could also be seen to indicate the complex changes taking place in the moral order of human society during the late middle ages. It was becoming more common to exhibit a degree of restraint in table manners that meant individuals were becoming more self-conscious and aware of how their own behavior affected others. Eating too quickly, spitting out unpalatable morsels and other such behavior was being recognized as repulsive to others.

The culinary world of the Renaissance was part of a comprehensive break with medieval traditions that cannot be decisively linked to any particular moment in time but became visible in the evolving changes in habits of consumption. The categorization systems of the middle ages were dominated by Aristotelian logic. The five human senses of sight, touch, hearing, taste and smell were strictly ranked with the visual at the highest level and smell and taste at the lowest. This hierarchical system relegated food to a lowly status as it was directly involved with the baser business of bodily maintenance. The visual, in contrast, was elevated as it encouraged the individual to look beyond the immediate to the heavens and the horizon, to search for abstract and more transcendental ideals. For many, this meant that how one consumed food was not strictly governed by rules of decorum. Eating was a matter of meeting a physical need, but with the growth of commerce and travel that brought strangers together in closer confines, the need to not offend became more urgent. Slowly, customs in table manners and rules about sharing food became more dominated by the need to avoid giving offence, particularly as the recently encountered stranger may shortly become a source of useful information or business. Trade then disturbed the Aristotelian universe and the sensory experiences of taste and smell were no longer being relegated to the lowest ranks of human experience.

Changes in social customs are not readily dated and do not appear to hinge on specific events or exact circumstances. Over time, there are discernible shifts that change the order of practices, and as they fluidly move between high and low, it is possible to see how new customs emerge. Such changes have a slow evolution, but once commenced they begin to reverberate in other spheres. For instance, changes in physical appearance, in the ways the body and its nutrition were thought about, changed markedly with the dissolution of rigid rankings based on the humoral model. No longer was the body a pre-ordained vessel; it was, instead, a scaffold on which to display power, taste and status. The use of fashions in appearance shaped ways of acting and seeing. The habits and interests of one sphere of activity thus seeped into others, and the Italian Renaissance provides spectacular instances where conventions were shifting and different social styles were emerging. In painting, for example, new techniques broke with tradition and subtly destabilized previous systems. Examples of this appeared in unexpected combinations with commodities that ranked at different levels that, in effect, mixed the base with the elevated. Still life paintings of flowers, rounds of bread, wine jars, bunches of grapes, lemons, fruit and bowls appeared (not for the first time, as Hellenic mosaics and wall paintings used these motifs) as evidence of a shift away from religious subjects to the properties of the visible world upon which new empires, such as the Dutch, were being founded (Gombrich 1960: 431). Still life paintings were increasingly popular with the wealthy urbane classes from the mid-seventeenth century as they represented the civil society they had built (Portús 2012: 184). Other changes in commercial transactions such as banking and trade would also create new patterns of thinking that in time influenced the development of more complex social forms such as class mobility, secularism and the protocols of the public sphere.

THE FOOD ECONOMY

Seventeenth-century Europe saw an explosion of interest in consumable products, especially coffee, tea and sugar (Mintz 1985). As an example of the rapid changes in tastes, Mintz cites the popularity of sugar in England. He estimated that from the 1660s to 1740s, consumption increased sevenfold and has continued to increase into the present. As well as sugar, the consumption of coffee and tea spread quickly through Great Britain and Western Europe and these appear to be the first edible luxuries that were, over a short time-span, made available to masses of people. They were also the first substances to become the basis of advertising campaigns to increase consumption (Mintz 1997: 359). The history of sugar from a luxury and medical antidote to a relatively cheap source of energy and food substitute in the eighteenth century, and a staple in everyone's diet by the next century, reflects the capacity of food customs to shift social values on a grand scale. Mintz observed that as consumption of sugar grew, so too did the industrial capacity to manufacture new food substances such as sugared fruits, then jams and marmalades. Integral to the development of new food products were new ways of thinking about daily life itself, from the investment of time in food preparation to the embellishment of specific foods with symbolic meanings and character. Mintz (1997: 364) has considered it puzzling that substances with no nutritional value such as tea, coffee, nutmeg, ginger, pepper and tobacco were popular and quickly absorbed into the daily diet and have remained so into the present time. Such trends demonstrate how the symbolic value of commodities does not necessarily equate with their natural properties.

To some extent, changes in cultural gravity explain shifts in consumer tastes. By the close of the seventeenth century, the market place and public domain had shifted attention away from the exclusivity of the court society to the city. In London, there was a bustling street life and shops along The Strand and Piccadilly were flourishing. Theaters, coffee houses and galleries were creating the atmosphere of a fashionable metropolis. This new dimension of street life provided abundant entertainment and opportunities for mingling social pleasures with commerce (Porter 2000: 36–7). Tastes for sugar and tobacco were influenced by such fashions, and the wider consumption of similar goods was encouraged by their increasing availability.

The connections between self-identity, city life and the importance of taste are well illustrated by the mass migration movements of the nineteenth and twentieth centuries, in which the host country in many instances struggled to resist the introduction of new practices and habits brought with migration. Often beliefs about ethnic identity and nationalism characterized these events, arousing both prejudice and hostility. For example, with the migration of Italians to Chicago in the late nineteenth century, there was a struggle to reform food habits that were perceived by members of the American host society as damaging to the health of the migrants, which in turn posed a threat to the wider social body. Harvey Levenstein (1988) has described this apparent cultural war as a struggle, in part, between traditional folkways and the developing scientization of commercialized mass-produced foods. He noted the remarkable success that the Italian cuisine has had upon contemporary American tastes while other migrant cuisines have had much less impact. The pizza, for instance, and spaghetti and meatballs are now staples of the American diet, and while the reproduction of these dishes may be unlike their home-grown counterparts, they are nonetheless enduring examples of foreign dishes that have entered the American food vernacular. Other cuisines such as Jewish and Chinese entered into the American home, but in a more bowdlerized form. The Italian cuisine has kept its style largely intact. This is all the more remarkable as it was the focus of a campaign by American reformers in the nineteenth century to change the eating habits of the newly arrived Italians. The reasons behind this effort were ostensibly benevolent; that is, they were directed at improving the living conditions and general health of the migrants who congregated in densely populated tenements in inner city areas. However, the Italian diet survived the reforming zeal of the emerging profession of American nutritionists due in part to strong family traditions and long-held regional recipes. It was also the case that the migrant enclaves contained their own shops and this encouraged the purchase of familiar products. The Italian diet was also slightly cheaper and the recently arrived migrant was financially unable to adopt the American diet – a factor largely overlooked by the professional nutritionists who also disparaged the Italian cuisine of putting meat, beans, cheese and pasta together as they considered such cooking destroyed food values.

The home economists employed by American government agencies were largely unsuccessful at getting Italians to change their food habits of preserving and bottling the staple ingredients such as tomatoes, cauliflowers, olives and grapes. These same reforming nutritionists were also impelled to establish their own legitimate expertise and professionalism. Yet by 1918, international politics had begun to exert different influences on domestic perspectives about food and diet. As food shortages and rations were affecting the availability of meats, the cuisine of Italy, which was an American ally in the First World War, became a popular solution. Pasta, rice and vegetables cooked in combination with meat was now being championed as an effective way of rationing in accord with government food restrictions. While it was the case that before the First World War, Italian migrants were disparaged for their frugality with food, these attitudes changed. Now their use of olive oil, cheese and vegetables was applauded. Ironically, by the early 1920s, with new research into nutrition and the discovery of vitamins, the conventional Italian diet was recognized as being well-balanced and rich in energy. The food reformers of the previous decade were compelled to revise their attitudes towards the imported dietary regime as pasta, tomatoes and meat sauce had become widely adopted staples.

Levenstein's study is an interesting example of how food fashions emerge and evolve not arbitrarily or inexplicably but most decidedly in concert with socio-economic and political influences. In America, a nascent concern with food and its effect on sensibilities had been strengthening since the marketing in 1829 of the Graham cracker or honey "bisket". Developed by Sylvester Graham, this bland biscuit was intended to disseminate Graham's puritanical beliefs that a strict and simple diet could control unhealthy bodily appetites and desires. Food was a matter of moral concern and connected directly to the individual's spiritual health. Graham's religious and health beliefs gained popularity and, in the next generation, they formed a more porous connection between diet, morality and the new industrial techniques of mass production. The Kellogg saga exemplifies the commercial opportunities seen in linking food and appetite with moral development. Like Sylvester Graham, John and Will Kellogg regarded food as integral to physical and spiritual health. In the 1890s, they established the Sanitas Food Company (the forerunner of the global Sanitarium brand) that marketed grains and cereals as a vegetarian breakfast substitute for the more costly meal of meat and eggs. Again, religious overtones can be seen in their attitudes to the disciplined body. They opened a health farm based on the Kellogg philosophy that advocated eliminating meat from the diet and regularly cleansing the intestinal tract with yoghurt and enemas. This was suggested as the best way to control unruly carnal desires. It assumed that natural bodily urges were ungovernable and needed to be contained. A bland diet was necessary in order to purify the body. Such attitudes place full responsibility on the individual for the nature of their appetites and desires, and intensify a sense of anxiety about the body as a potential source of unwanted disclosure and betrayal. If the individual eschewed this attention to health and continued to consume exotic substances, they could be seen as degenerate, decadent and even diseased. The motif of purity in the maintenance of the physical body took on a more sinister political inflection when used to support racial segregation and the virtue of eugenics. The older Kellogg brother, John, wrote popular texts on how to live a good life that included ideas sympathetic to racial purification. In the changing economic and political circumstances of America in the early twentieth century, it was easy to elide concerns with health and personal hygiene with a broader social frame that focused on the strength and vitality of the body politic.

Anxieties about food and health have not disappeared or even lessened in the present. The food scares of the 1980s and 1990s (salmonella-contaminated eggs and

BSE – bovine spongiform encephalopathy – transmitted through contaminated beef) have had an impact on customer needs for quality assurance. An increased regulatory environment has emerged and been imposed on the agents along the food supply chain, with varying degrees of success. Now foods are packaged with information on some of the sources of their ingredients in order to provide customers with reassurance about freshness and the origins of the product. Fresh foods such as meat, fish and cheese sold directly across a shop counter are not always seen as having the same quality assurance that packaged foods can display with use-by-dates and labelled nutritional information. The transparent plastic, vacuum-packed food – such as high-quality cut meat or fish – has increased the purchase price of the item and has been a marketing success in terms of increasing customer up-take. As food is continuously being rebranded, re-evaluated and repackaged, it directly influences the patterns of our eating habits.

Developing tastes for certain products is part of food marketing. Marion Nestle (2002: 1) has pointed out that on a global scale, "food companies must convince people to eat more of their products". They are active in developing fads and fashions in consumer tastes. While the popularity of consumer items may appear directly connected to changed methods in advertising such as product placement in the movies as early as 1958 with the Kleenex box in the Hollywood rom-com movie *Indiscreet*, and music video clips (celebrity endorsements of Pepsi, Lucozade, milk), there are other factors such as agricultural practices and technological advances in manufacture that also create demand for novel tastes. Shifts in contemporary tastes are frequently linked to marketing cycles that are further connected to supply chains in related industries where technological innovations in manufacture have also exerted an influence on food production. The popularity of items such as sweetened drinks, ice cream, baked biscuits, pre-prepared and frozen meals are all part of larger industrial processes that have successfully positioned supply before demand and cultivated markets for certain tastes. In the new techniques used in milk production, for instance, the collection of the by-product whey has enabled an increase in the production of yoghurt which in recent years has become a popular health food and generated a sizeable new market.

The supermarket has played a critical role in the transformation of food and, in turn, our eating habits. It has been as important to food consumption as the department store was in the mid-nineteenth century to the democratization of fashion. In the supermarket, the consumer helps themselves to products. As in the department store, there is no barrier between the product and purchaser. Previously, the convention was for a customer to transact with a shopkeeper across a counter and this invoked both social as well as physical barriers. The opportunity to handle goods, to touch, hold and examine them immediately establishes a more emotionally charged and intimate relationship. In the early department store, this was a factor in rapidly increasing sales. Once the customer has held the luxury object, felt the quality of the leather gloves, smelled the perfume of the cosmetics, tied a silk scarf around the neck, it became much harder to return it to the display shelves.

Similarly, in the supermarket, the distance has collapsed and we are commonly much more engaged in choosing food items and reading their ingredients and pedigree from the ubiquitous label. Previously, many foods were held in bulk, and the grocer or shopkeeper wrapped and packaged the amounts of food requested. The revolutionary changes brought about by the supermarket have appeared to empower the customer who can now stroll the shelves of stacked foods and select whatever they want. This provides a sense of freedom that has led shoppers to handle and select products that appeal not necessarily as staple items but as amusements and novelties. Strolling the shelves of brightly colored and cleverly packaged goods is a type of *flâneurship*.

The supermarket has brought together a wide range of goods that captures our attention and provides for every taste. It commonly contains chilled and frozen ready-to-eat meals alongside an endless array of raw ingredients; it offers cheaper house-style products as well as imported novelties; it markets both staples and luxuries. It appears to provide an open, tantalizing bazaar of products that suggests we have unfettered choice. By definition, supermarkets sell almost everything from staples to luxuries, from food to electric light bulbs. They invite the consumer to stroll along the aisles following the logic of the goods on display, finding items that seem to hang together – laundry items with cleaners and paper goods, fresh meats alongside raw vegetables and cheeses. There appears to be no sinister design to promote suggestive selling in this layout; only the convenient arrangement of related goods.

Yet the supermarket is a highly engineered place that maximizes selling. It has provided a stimulus to the food packaging industries as it constantly encourages the introduction of new foods that are presented in attractively designed packages that not only improve shelf-life and prevent deterioration but also increase the number of products on display. Shopping in the supermarket has turned products into entertainments. Food is now packaged along with further advertised offers for various competitions and special purchases. There are well-branded foods that appeal to us on the basis of a trusted brand name; there are new lines of foods such as diet products, health foods and no-frill home brands that promise quality without the hidden costs of add-on advertising. Packaging has changed our perceptions. The once trusted tin container that was hermetically sealed and guaranteed to keep its contents wholesome even after a long shelf-life has been replaced by packaging that is softer, more palpable and makes the food contents more visible.

The concept of the self-service grocery may have been the invention of an American entrepreneur, Clarence Saunders, in the second decade of the twentieth century, but the present growth of the supermarket has been tied to other economic conditions. It was well established in America before Tesco emerged as the leading supermarket retailer in Britain and Coles in Australia during the 1960s. Since then, the marketing of comestibles has become more intertwined with the continuous creation of new tastes based on the "science" of marketing. Supermarkets now employ a variety of technologies designed to influence the shopper and subtly shape our sense of freedom of choice. Self-scanning that is offered as a way of avoiding the checkout queue and loyalty cards that reward the high consumer also gather a great deal of data about our purchasing preferences. Such information can be used to develop shopper profiles that are deemed useful for directing sales information in more personalized and targeted campaigns. Supermarkets, homeware stores and shopping malls also provide *crèches*, coffee shops, pharmacists and delivery services that all enhance the shopping experience.

Recently, the US-based grocery chain Wal-Mart has been named the "corporate gorilla" that has replaced General Motors as the largest retail business on the planet. It employs 1.4 million people: a workforce that is larger than General Motors, Ford, General Electric and IBM combined. Its annual revenue is 2 percent of the US GDP (Head 2003). Wal-Mart is a hypermart that sells more than groceries; it sells services such as medical care, insurance, car maintenance and so on. It began in the mid-twentieth century as a bargain store aimed at women on low incomes. Originally, the store was housed in an "ugly box-shaped building" in rural towns with populations of less than 5,000 people. This was an effective business strategy as it established monopolies in small markets and ensured success without the competitive presence of larger retailers. Wal-Mart has since expanded at a rapid rate and drawn the attention of high-end business and labor analysts who marvel at its rapid success. Its economic growth has been directly linked with its stringent employment practices that have produced numerous long-standing lawsuits alleging sex discrimination and harsh payment structures. It has been alleged that a full-time sales clerk at Wal-Mart earns below the official American government's definition of the poverty line (Head 2003: 4f). The supermarket, well illustrated in the history of Wal-Mart, in combination with the globalization of consumer products, reinforces the view that food is effective in conveying limitless messages that describe its consumers as well as the commercial framework in which industry and corporate interests are mutually advantaged.

When we choose to shop at Lidl, Sainsbury's, Kroger, Coles or A&P, we may do so for the convenience but also for the amorphous add-ons suggested by reputation. It is not possible to know whether a preference for a particular grocery store, high street restaurant, type of car, chocolate bar, brand of vodka and so on is governed more by cultural practices that have taken root in our consumer consciousness, or from well-exercised critical interrogation that informs our everyday actions. Resolving this question hardly matters when we consider that the currency around the ideas of free will, identity, self-expression and selfhood is so deeply inserted in everyday discourse that its unanswered presence is taken for granted. As a matter of course, in everyday life, whether we are immediately conscious of it or not, we animate deeply encoded meanings of the prevailing culture. In our preferences and performances, we are informed by instructive prescriptions that are constantly delivered to us through popular forms of address. The consumer ethic is paradoxical insofar as it constantly invites us to buy identity through commodities that continuously re-figure us with attractive new qualities and aspirations. The commerce in identity is comprehensive and the mystery of identity is so familiar it almost disappears. It is in such terms that Eva Illouz (2007) understands the mechanics of emotional capitalism.

Identity is reconstructed on a daily basis by adding emotional coloration. In various forms we are constantly interrogated about our preferences and desires: do we like what we are doing – are we bored? Why not take a break and buy a holiday, chocolate bar or new perfume? It is not that emotions drive us to action, and that the intensity of the emotion underlying our actions is the measure of our selfhood; rather it is the unreflected nature of our actions that measures the emotional investment. Emotions are compressed into consciousness and actions to provide texture and granularity. Thus we act in order to maintain emotional equilibrium and to secure those valued feelings of comfort and assurance. These ideas resonate with Roland Barthes (1972) when he describes how ideas that are most readily accepted as self-evident and neutral truths are better thought of as being the expression of a successfully introjected culture. Whatever seems unremarkable, ordinary and natural is a measure of the depth of cultural immersion. The acceptance of identity as problematic, as constantly in need of definition, development, expression and improvement, has assumed this level of importance – it is a fact of modern life – and by accepting its centrality, the mythologies of its nature and needs are at their most potent.

TASTE AND LONGING

All tastes are acquired. The taste for refined objects is cultivated, as is the taste for flavor. Taste refers to preferences for artichokes, shellfish, coffee and tobacco but also tastes in possessions and practices. Taste in all its variety has long been regarded as a symbol of refinement and politeness that gives definition to personal identity. Since the seventeenth century, taste has been a contested concept, yet it is in everyday use as a means of categorizing people and their habits (Bourdieu 1984: 2). How we handle objects and instruments such as cups and saucers, knives and forks has imposed a mannered overlay on the body and, to those watching, our deftness with such objects translates into a measure of prized personal attributes. The habits we develop for eating, drinking, standing, moving and living are used to reflect aspects of personal character. These instances of mastery, or lack of, are recognized by others (and ourselves) as displays of competency and discernment; our gestures, the way we gaze, how we hold eye contact, the timbre of our accent, the strength of our voice are all used as indices to identity.

The concept of taste has come to be a shortcut estimation of personal qualities. Yet this late seventeenth-century idea becomes inversely useful as a social yardstick for categorizing others at the same time that material goods are more readily available. As we begin to own an ever-multiplying number of goods, these possessions become less reliable as indicators of class and social distinction. A more subtle form of discrimination is necessary that relies less on the ownership of goods and more on the types of goods we own. Taste transcends the financial cost of possession and supplies instead a reason for selecting one item over another from a wide range of functionally indistinguishable options. Taste becomes the vital ingredient in the demonstration of social distinction. In *The Portrait of a Lady* (James 1881), the European aristocrats Gilbert Osmond and Serena Merle present themselves as the epitome of good taste; they demonstrate that taste and identity are inseparable: "(the self) flows into everything that belongs to us – and then it flows back again. I know a large part of myself is in the clothes I choose to wear. I've a great respect for *things!*" Madame Merle goes on to list the house and its furnishings, the books she reads and the friends she associates with as indicative of her fine character (Thomas 2009: 129–31).

The exercise of taste brings attention to different types of desire. Pursuing an experience for its own sake because, say, it is pleasing or reassuring or elevating, and pursuing a desire in order to gratify it and make it disappear, are two different impulses. The former involves detachment, of being able to recognize value in an idea without it having an immediate application; the latter is a more active process in which the desirable has to be devoured and captured in some way in order to nullify its insistence. For example, food can be valued for its aesthetic qualities or it can be treated as a fuel to stem the spasms of hunger. It can have appeal as the subject for a still life painting, as in the masterpieces of Caravaggio and Luis Meléndez or with Elizabeth David's description of the cobalt blue cabbages on display in the early morning Venetian market, where it successfully evokes our aesthetic responses. Being able to see its multidimensionality is itself a demonstration of cultural distinction. The popular view of the restaurant as part of the entertainment industries and one of the many conveniences of modern metropolitan life underplays its importance. Yet to view the restaurant from a distance, with detachment, and to separate it from the conveniences of everyday life, is to recognize that it is more than it seems. The restaurant has exaggerated the meaning of food; it has emphasized style and separated form from function. The restaurant defines food as more than bodily fuel and in so doing it enables us to overlay our appetites with sublimated desires. Nestle (2000) and Foer (2009) re-cast food as global politics, Lévi-Strauss (1969) and Goody (1982) as the essence of cultural difference, Norbert Elias (1978) as an ingredient in the civilizing process, Bourdieu (1984) as an expression of class position. When we separate food from physical need, we produce a wider horizon for understanding its meaning.

The idea of taste is widely contested, but in the early modern period it was a reliable index of the "polite" and it was expressed by those who belonged to an elite. Taste was obvious; it rested on ownership of certain goods and the display of expert knowledge about why such goods were to be admired. It was the prerogative of those with taste to display it in much the same way we might now think it is the prerogative of the celebrity to flaunt wealth. Bourdieu (1984: 2) has demonstrated in his contemporary study of the French middle classes that while taste may be a contested concept, it is in daily use as a means for categorizing people and their habits. As social mobility slowly increased during the seventeenth and eighteenth centuries, the display of taste became a commodity that the new rich could purchase. When the *nouveaux riches* emerged as a social class, they emulated the lifestyles of their social superiors and in time challenged their status. The new rich could look like aristocrats and buy the necessary paraphernalia that displayed equivalent power and status; they could purchase the signs of superiority and discernment and indeed they generated a market in experts who could train them in the demonstration of the finer qualities. These experts included gardeners, artists, architects and so on, who styled the houses of the arrivistes and filled them with the requisite objects.

With the wider distribution of wealth and the growing success of new social classes appearing to be cultured, the measures of taste narrowed; it became necessary to sharpen the definition from the "conspicuous display of opulence to a more restrained demonstration of elegance, refinement and fastidious discrimination" (Thomas 2009: 129). When taste was applied to an object, it was visible, but when individuals were claiming an elevated personal status on the basis of their own good taste, its definition was more esoteric and obscure. Social superiority displayed through taste was associated with specific types of education and worldly experience. In this sense, it was less tangible; it could be displayed in the seemingly ordinary practice of purchasing a piece of ribbon or in the number of buttons displayed on a jacket cuff. In some social circles, during periods of high social mobility in the late eighteenth and early nineteenth centuries, it was important to be dressed appropriately. As a sign of good taste, Richard Sennett has described how the least incongruity in appearance and style could be interpreted as a telltale detail that warned others of a lurking barbarity. The assumptions behind such a view were drawn from the popular physiognomists of the previous century such as Johann Caspar Lavater (1741–1801), who had demonstrated that every element of conduct and appearance revealed hidden dimensions of character. It was socially de rigueur to be highly aware of details, after the deductive manner of the popular fictional detective Sherlock Holmes. Raw human nature needed to be governed; there was always a risk it could erupt at any time and destroy the fragile boundary between civility and social chaos. People came to regard one another's appearance and behavior as clues to this possibility. Thus the signs of character, status and identity of the upper classes became evident, for example, in a jacket where the buttons on the cuff actually buttoned and unbuttoned (Sennett 1976: 166).

As the purchasing power of the new middle classes expanded, the exercise of taste went beyond wealth. In the mid-twentieth century, in an era of tightening conformity and new bourgeois values, Russell Lynes (1949) famously defined taste along three dimensions – highbrow, lowbrow and middle brow – alluding to the physiognomic interpretation of the high aristocratic forehead and the low forehead of the beast. Taste became the new social hierarchy and cultural capital came to rest on speech patterns, vocabulary, mannerisms, emotional responses and ideas. Such opaque ways of judging one another were part of the bloodless revolution in which taste became a new form of social engineering. A consequence of this revolution was to inaugurate a regime of continual status panic; according to C.W. Mills (1951), the middle classes became caught in a constant re-positioning of themselves within an ever-shifting mobile hierarchy defined by fashion and opinion. Of this era, Dwight MacDonald (1944: 22) quipped that a person of taste was someone who could look at a sausage and think of Picasso.

This shift in sensibility from quantity to quality, from matter to manner, meant that meals were judged not on the number of overflowing dishes but on the choice of meats, the delicacy of the seasoning, the courtesy with which the repast was served. In styles of dress, too, excess was being admonished; the display of jewellery was abjured for the more subtle displays of tasteful fashions in tailoring. Taste was an index to position and value in a social universe that was becoming more fluid and indecipherable: "in modern times, there is nothing which more exactly defines social differences than personal tastes, whether in food or music or wallpaper or the choice of children's names. The choices which people make in these areas of life may seem spontaneous and genuine but, without any apparent pressure or coercion, they usually conform to class lines. The possessions which we place in our living spaces and the way we decorate those spaces instantly reveal our sensibilities, our preoccupations, and our social milieux" (Thomas 2009: 132).

The rules for eating documented by Fernand Braudel (1973) and Norbert Elias (1978), such as the admonitions not to eat hungrily, not to gulp food and not to spit out gristly morsels, illustrate the requirement to distance oneself from the act of eating and by doing so demonstrate an elevated social status. Developing tastes for certain practices, including tastes in appetite, is still associated with social distinctions. Perhaps not with a clear sense of class, but now more closely aligned with materialism, popular culture and membership to particular social networks. Taste can be a measure of distance from the quotidian; it measures exclusivity and esoteric specialist knowledge. It works with preferences in food; new tastes are constantly becoming fashionable – virgin olive oil in preference to unsalted butter; Italian Prosecco more than French Champagne; fish not red meat; sorbet not ice cream, and so on. In the modern consumerist society, where all manner of entertainments and pleasures can be purchased, the restaurant has become an arbiter of taste; it has separated the consumer into different types and generated an economy around styles in food that in turn supports a proliferation of commercial interests.

The greater availability of material goods and entertaining pleasures in the present society has brought more attention to the types of distinction that can differentiate our preferences. A connection is posited by merchandizers and consumers alike that certain goods equate with types of subjectivity. Commodities become imbued with human qualities and we, in turn, become their embodiments – the Marlboro man, Pepsi tribe, Nike team and so on. At the same time that preferences distinguish us and create an image that others can read, they also make taste a more difficult category to define. As Keith Thomas has described, the idea is applied liberally but its explanatory power to account for our peculiar manners of acting remains tied to stereotypes. Even as taste refers to seemingly idiosyncratic preferences such as liking McDonald's hamburgers and Nike trainers and Ferrari cars and seventeenth-century Dutch paintings, the question still remains whether the concept has enough explanatory power to convey useful information. Such odd concatenations of preferences may describe little more than promiscuity with current fads *à la mode*.

If we accept that consumption provides a lifestyle, then products are seen to have the capacity to illuminate personal details. The consuming of goods and services becomes a way of absorbing values and clichés from the external social context into an internal coherence. In the early work of Raymond Williams (1961), he argued that understanding social patterns and habits of living required attention to a layer of meaning he referred to as "the structure of feeling". Williams pointed out that how we think and feel about ourselves and others plays a singularly important role in shaping the way we choose to live.

To better understand the nature of everyday life, we need to look beyond social institutions such as the family and the organization of economic production; we need to understand the desires we develop, how they are communicated to others, what kinds of pleasures we pursue. This emphasis on the feeling structure of everyday life informs the value we accord commodities and further illustrates some of the mechanics of emotional capitalism (Illouz 1997).

IDENTITY FOR SALE

Styles of consumption may well contribute to the formation of our subjectivity, to how we think of ourselves and the world we inhabit, yet the nature of the consumer in the globalized economy is constantly shifting. We are often portrayed as passive but restless, bored and anxious, as someone who needs the goods offered by advertisers and marketers in order to claim a sense of purpose. Mid-twentieth century, Vance Packard offered a strong argument about how easily consumers were influenced in their consumer habits. In *The Hidden Persuaders* (1957), he described how advertising companies were deliberately using psychological techniques to manipulate our desires. This approach was immediately popular as consumers responded to the idea that human psychology could be unconsciously manipulated. In a way, this made people less responsible for their unnecessary purchases. A more contemporary but still critical portrait of the consumer is provided by Dick Hebdige (1993: 82), who describes the ideal consumer as a complete social and psychological mess, as a decentered subject who is a bundle of conflicting drives and fantasies and who is, as a result, passive, irresponsible, unanchored and unreliable. Lauren Langman (2009: 472) adds to the view by suggesting that the privatized hedonism of the contemporary consumer has an enfeebled self-identity hidden behind a plurality of masks drawn from popular culture. Our shifting desires form the essence of a de-essentialized self (Brown 2003: 213). Thus my pursuit of certain satisfactions produces in turn an assemblage I call identity that has been fragmented to the point of decimation. We are capable of being dozens of different characters as we habitually come to occupy an array of diverse subject positions made visible to us in certain popular entertainments and fashionable commodities. Thus my idiosyncratic preferences for junk food and high culture, for French fries and Vermeer paintings, have little significance as I am constantly replacing these preferences with new ones. As a result, we find an appealing degree of psychological comfort in automaton-like conformity to an ever-shifting array of experiences. While I am both capable of and pleased with my capacity to extract pleasure from eating junk food, watching Hollywood blockbuster movies, following serialized soap operas on television and buying brand name trainers, I am equally reassured that such behavior means little as it can be so easily changed.

The value placed on self-fashioning and reinvention has had a relatively short but incisive history. It highlights the irresolvable debate between the opposed positions, on the one hand, of defining the self as an essential interior core reflected in reliable expressions of physiognomy, and on the other, that identity is not a human universal but more accurately a modern Western concept that has been naturalized and made into a universal idea. The idea of self-identity is paradoxical; it supposedly encapsulates individuality, of how we feel different and separate from others, but it also inserts us into a collective identity that provides a sense of belonging. The conceptualization of identity took an abrupt turn in the eighteenth century with the rise of the popular novel and the strengthening of secularism. Thereafter, the idea of identity became more obviously imbued with cultural practices that generate a diffuse and ambiguous definition. However, the concept of personal identity remains popular even as we recognize that its presumed constituents of deep emotions, memories and expressions of interiority elude stable definition. The mystery content of the self allows for considerable confusion over the origins of influential imperatives and values and whether they have emanated from external ideological interests in commerce, nationalism, religion, gender and class or are part of the inherent qualities of a coherent, essential self.

Consumerism emphasizes the meaningfulness of objects. Food, cars, types of leisure activities, political positions and business ethics are constantly being re-valued, re-appropriated and rebranded in terms of how they contribute to personal identity. Dining at the gastronomic pinnacle of a Michelin three-star restaurant, buying an electric car and Fair Trade bananas can be the signs of an ethical consumer who appreciates the demands of a greener civic society; at the same time, such a consumer can appear to be the opposite — privileged and indulgent. The consumer era has increased the density of the material culture in which we live, thus providing us with more to choose from but at the same time increasing the desire for wanting more without fixing any parameters of surfeit. Thus we arrive at a point where we are seeking to maximize our consumer pleasures, to meet our desires and fulfil our tastes by imbuing our preferred commodities with personal meaning, with an aura that reflects back on us, thus showing others who we are through our possessions and displays of taste.

The idea that we are complicit in our own subjugation to these consumerist imperatives is unpopular and is readily countered by instances where other preoccupations such as family and friendships, participating in civic discourses and working for a vocation are depicted as affording more reliable pleasures in a self-directed, autonomous life. Such a view supports a belief in a stable self where our consciousness is not colonized by consumer desires but is rather actively engaged in asserting our independence from economic or political interests that would otherwise make us automaton consumers. As modern consumers, we do traverse a wide horizon of possible subjective states, sometimes being a dupe of the marketing industries and at other times an astute advocate of responsible consumption. We might well understand consumption as being the final act in a long chain of connections linking central government policies with international trade agreements and legally regulated social obligations of global corporations but, at the same time, we also understand it as an immediate source of private pleasure. In whatever guise, it is evident that our relationship to commodities, to the abundance of things manufactured in the modern era, is a site where interests are contested. We have emotional investments in relationships with people as much as we do with inanimate objects. Bourdieu (1984) has illustrated this with his empirical study of the French middle classes, in which he described the nature of the modern consumer by aligning choices in lifestyles with economic, religious, cultural and symbolic indicators. He mapped taste by identifying who purchased branded goods, owned a sports car, married young, had a mortgage, took exotic vacations, ate fish and green vegetables more often than meat and potatoes and, on this basis, has argued for the need to cultivate a more detached and dispassionate perspective on consumerism in general.

We are familiar with the idea that we have relationships with objects and that we understand ourselves within an environment crowded with heavily branded commodities. We also know that the presentation of the self in everyday life is ambiguous (Goffman 1961). We are constantly concerned with crafting impressions and controlling the messages we may inadvertently "give off". Into this arena comes the appearance of stability of meaning expressed through objects themselves. Branded goods appear to have desirable properties that we can adopt and attach to ourselves. When we buy Levi's, Calvin Klein, Bulgari, Missoni, Diesel and so on, we are buying more than the product. The characterization of these branded goods has been so strong that it creates an aura that extends beyond their material boundaries. If we favor Grolsch over Bud, Dior over Max Factor, Paul Smith over George, then we are expressing a self-image through the commodity. Ironically, the signature identity of the branded product itself is always shifting as its designers continually proliferate its application in order to increase sales. Branded goods multiply. Pierre Cardin was an early innovator of contiguous branding; his initial success with clothing soon widened to other goods. This collaboration across categories has become the norm; Dolce & Gabbana endorse clothes, motorbike helmets and also sponsor a football club, Armani has perfume, wrist watches and a hotel or two, Prada lent its name to a mobile phone, Ferragamo has a network of boutique hotels, Hermès has entered the market of art galleries and museums. In these instances, the branded product has acquired a multiplicity of identities, extending its original symbolic value. Purchasing a social identity and self-image through a heavily branded object has become a conventional practice of everyday life. Our consumer patterns fit us into a particular category on the socio-economic spectrum according to class, age, gender, income, education and location even though we probably prefer to think of ourselves as embodiments of finer, more abstract qualities found in cultivated tastes and values.

To better understand the consumer society requires an active denaturalization of all that seems obvious. The exhaustive surveys and reports of who does what to whom, when and where, provide evidence of distinctions, of how we differ from others and claim a sense of uniqueness. However, to accept that embedded in every ritual, habit and social act there is a re-statement of personal identity is to accept as well that the process of interiorizing sensations and emotions is socially and historically circumstantial. How the various incidental connections are formed and activated produces and continuously reproduces a sense of biographical coherence that we understand as identity. Throughout the everyday, this process of constituting ourselves continues as we pursue desires, formulate tastes and experiment with needs. We are agents in this process, as are the more abstract influences of commercial, political and economic institutions. A closer look at everyday habits and seemingly ordinary practices such as where and what we eat can provide enough detachment from our habits to enable us to consider how tastes and appetites, beyond those for food preferences, have been fashioned.

"I suppose I should have let a few minutes elapse between declaring my love for you and announcing that I also loved lobster."

Cartoon by J.B. Handelsman, published 5 January 1987

(THE NEW YORKER)

3   EATING HABITS

The restaurant does not have a singular character; the most basic of its functions is to deliver food at the request of a paying customer. From there, it reproduces itself in myriad forms. Restaurants differ most obviously from each other in terms of their costs, reputation and status and hours of business; they are most similar to one another in their recognition of decor and ambience as essential ingredients in the pleasure of dining. The proliferation of the restaurant's form has not obeyed any definable and orderly principles; its success is part of the explosion of human tastes and social activities that have come to characterize the modern liberal era. The different kinds of dining out discussed below are not mutually exclusive; a spectacular restaurant in the category of *Fête Spéciale* does not always have a decor superior in its attention to detail to that found in the *bistro mondain*, nor does it always mean that such a restaurant is more popular with tourists than a themed restaurant. The quality of the food does not necessarily correspond with the decor and service. Exceptions exist, yet the typology is useful for highlighting similarities between restaurants as diverse as the McDonald's fast food outlet, the massive Mezzo with its 700 tables, the Sun Dial at the rotating top of Peach Tree Plaza, and the legendary Four Seasons.

The modern restaurant has evolved from a variety of antecedents such as cook shops, coffee houses, inns, guilds and fraternities, all of which had in common their location in the busy social arena where individuals were highly likely to encounter strangers. These public houses provided opportunities for indulging new gustatory tastes, say, for coffee and tobacco, as well as companionship and other private appetites. They functioned as laboratories for modernity insofar as they allowed individuals to act outside their given social positions, to seek entertainment and opportunities for social mobility. These new social arenas mostly brought men into contact with one another and encouraged social experimentation and competition (Thomas 2009: 225). Such cultural developments underlie a strong human impulse for sociability and the stimulation that comes from unexpected encounters. Zygmunt Bauman (2001) refers to such pleasures as fundamental to the human condition. Being sociable mobilizes a sense of agitation; it reflects an inability to be still and ignites the search for diversion and commotion in all our activities. Practices such as dining out illustrate this human trait through which we have learned to be sociable and exercise those capacities that build enough trust between individuals to support the basic ingredients of all social life.

CLASSIC STUDIES

An early study of dining out was *Human Relations in the Restaurant Industry* (1948) by William Foote Whyte. Researched in Chicago in the last years of the Second World War, the study was designed to stimulate and improve management processes but, at the same time, Whyte's sharp sociological eye provided insights into the working community within the restaurant including relations between waiters, chefs and clients. The management of status between them was a salient feature. He described the front and back stage of the restaurant and how it correlated with the degrees of mobility open to each of them. For instance, the chef and diner hold the highest status in the restaurant, and yet they are the most confined to a limited space and territory. In contrast, the waiter is at the beck and call of others and moves from dining room to kitchen and back again without much restriction. Service is of central importance to the pleasures of dining. Whyte described the exchange between the diner and service staff as being complex and fragile. While waiters can be thought of as employees of the diner in a sense, in practice they are more like directors of a theatrical performance; they are the *puppetmeister* who controls the tempo of the event. In the formal restaurant, the diner is highly dependent on the attention and service provided by the waiter. These have an immediate impact on the pleasures at the table. When there is no waiter – as in the fast food outlet – nonetheless, service remains important. It may be largely automated and part of the engineered physical space where face-to-face encounters are designed to be at a minimum, but that in itself has significance. The diner may choose the self-serving restaurant as a way of avoiding the waiter and the social tensions that are necessarily involved in the delivery of service. Whyte points out that the presence of the waiter heightened the expectations and the social complexities that confronted the diner. The waiter was the embodiment of the restaurant even as s/he appeared to be a servant (Whyte 1948: 24). The subtleties of this relationship influence the social maneuvers that take place within all types of restaurants, from the most formal to the local café on the high street.

Other classic ethnographic studies of the restaurant, such as *The Cocktail Waitress* (Spradley and Mann 1975) and *The*

World of Waiters (Mars and Nicod 1984), further support many of Whyte's observations and provide examples where the micro-practices within the restaurant can be regarded as extensions of those found in the world at large (see also Beriss and Sutton 2007). The reproduction of conventional gender roles is illustrated by Spradley and Mann, who focus on interactional rituals and how regular customers become part of a community. The cocktail waitress in this setting provides the social cohesion that encourages solidarity among regulars. She acts to make clients feel as if they belong as she understands and often anticipates their needs, thereby creating an inclusive, supportive atmosphere.

A sense of community in the restaurant has long been recognized as important. In the early nineteenth century, Jean Anthelme Brillat-Savarin made the prescient observation that when diners re-make the restaurant in their own image, their appetites are appeased. Re-territorializing the restaurant into a place of one's own, making it familiar and comfortable, is essential to the pleasure of dining out. This process is about mapping oneself onto a social territory and feeling as if one has some authority; at the same time, the restaurant must exert its own boundaries in order to manage the constant stream of strangers that it necessarily accommodates. The successful balancing of these different requirements characterizes the event.

Part of the dining experience engages us in self-fashioning as we test the immediate environment as being sympathetic to our choices. The waiter mirrors that process, tacitly informing us whether we are successful or not in claiming our desired public persona. Even though the waiter is a factotum, an instrument that is purchased along with the meal, the transaction is not straightforward. In a liberal society, the practices of rampant consumerism make the acquisition of goods an ordinary event, but when the purchase is human service, not a material commodity, then it involves a complicated psychological dimension. Purchasing human service exposes emotional investments involving trust and reciprocity. The transaction is dependent on subtle negotiations. The diner might commission the waiter, but it is the waiter who brings the event into production. As such, there is a constant interplay in which desires are exposed and addressed, and the balance of power shifts back and forth between the players. In the study by Mars and Nicod, the waiter is depicted as a knowing social actor who exercises a battery of "fiddles" that are designed ultimately to exploit the diner. These include the worst clichés of dining out – untouched food being returned to the kitchen and then re-used, special menus that feature food that needs to be thrown away if not immediately consumed, and padded bills with items not ordered by the diner. The role of the waiter remains central to the literal pleasure of dining. The attractive, flirtatious waiter provides the extra service of raising the emotional temperature in a restaurant by intensifying the expectation that all manner of pleasures will be met. Like the courtesan of the pre-modern Court Society, the waiter can create an atmosphere in which the individual feels important as every need and desire are cordially met. Even where there is no waiter in the self-service fast food chains or the local café, there is still a protocol that orders how we act and the degree of pleasure we can derive. The restaurant, in all its variety, is a meticulously engineered space.

INSIDE THE RESTAURANT

As a way of examining dining out, the typology of restaurants below highlights the diversity and general similarities.

Categorizing restaurants is an analytic convenience and there will always be exceptions; this attempt at systematization is only to identify those structural and commercial features that add to our understanding of the popularity of dining out in all its diversity. Media commentary and reviews of restaurants usually focus on service and decor, menu and cuisine, pricing and value for money, and to a lesser extent on location, clientele, and the degree of fame enjoyed by the resident chef. There is an emphasis too on the fashionability of the restaurant and the reliable entertainment it provides that makes dining out seem worthwhile. These same factors more or less guide the following analyses with an added focus on how dining out is absorbed into the everyday repertoire of behaviours that constitute our sense of social identity.

Spectacular	Engaging	Convenient
Fête Spéciale	Bistro Mondain	Café Mundane
Delmonico's	Boca di Lupo	Brunetti's
The Four Seasons	Momofuku	Sizzler
Stephanie's	Hard Rock Café	Bill's Garage
Per Se	Jamie's	KFC

The spectacular *Fête Spéciale*

Fête Spéciale is a spectacular restaurant distinguished by its cost and reputation. This invented term plays with the hegemony of French cuisine by inflecting the name with excessive accents. These restaurants can be exceptionally expensive, even when they are relatively informal. Such restaurants are globally common; they are found perched atop a high office tower or set in the refurbished elegance of a late nineteenth-century building. They commonly have personnel who are impressively tailored but whose personal conduct can be variable, even desultory. Their attraction is often location, decor and reputation. To dine out in such a restaurant is to pursue social aspirations; it is a place to go, such as Per Se (New York) and The Pearl (Mumbai). The cuisine of such restaurants is usually touted as superlative, but it can vary. Delmonico's, for example, one of the earliest of the spectacular restaurants, was more effective in creating the reputation of New York City at the turn of the twentieth century than it was a place to meet with gastronomic pleasures. Even with its celebrity chef, Charles Ranhofer, and its signature dishes, Delmonico's was a social scene more than a gustatory experience. In cosmopolitan cities, there are now six and seven star hotels that provide such restaurants where the costs are high and the food not necessarily as adventurous or skilfully prepared as can be found in select boutique bistros. Nonetheless, dining at a *Fête Spéciale* may be more about status and self-display than cuisine. Following Thorstein Veblen's theory of the leisure classes, dining in such places is a form of conspicuous consumption when the reputation and drama of the *Fête Spéciale* overshadow the actualities of sluggish table service, inflated prices and ordinary food styles. In the case of the famous tourist restaurant, dining out may be a matter of being able to say one has been there. This can be especially satisfying when table reservations at such a restaurant need to be made several months in advance.

Every large city in the Westernized world has at least one and probably five or six restaurants that are reputedly amongst the best in the world. Each has an impressive interior with elegant chairs, perhaps an exotic marble fireplace, huge crystal chandeliers and an unparalleled wine cellar. Each has a front manager with a charming manner, a chef with impeccable culinary experience and a sommelier with a vast knowledge of local and classic wines. These restaurants are deeply imbued with reputation.

The *Fête Spéciale* rarely creates an intimate, warm atmosphere but is more likely to be grand in scale with some intention to overwhelm. The spectacular restaurant emphasizes its physical setting as part of its attraction. These restaurants give access to places we might not otherwise frequent such as the 35th floor of a city skyscraper with 360-degree views, a 300-year-old vineyard or a picturesque coastal working harbor. Much of their success depends upon the entertainment provided by these features, but another important element is that the diners themselves are on display. The attraction of taking tea at The Ritz is to be served in an open and highly visible setting and to watch the panorama of others doing the same.

Some of these spectacular restaurants provide casual meals and cocktails to their more transient but well-heeled clients. For example, the Sun Dial restaurant rotating on the pinnacle of the Peach Tree Plaza in Atlanta, Georgia provides a 360-degree view of the city and surrounding countryside with its incongruous Stony Mountain on the horizon. It seats approximately 300 people and has a classic menu known as international style and is comparatively expensive. This description would also fit similar restaurants such as The Summit atop Australia House in Sydney and others in the grandeur of the Hyatt Regency Hotels in Dallas, San Francisco and Birmingham, UK. The *Fête Spéciale* with a unique setting that cannot be imitated uses this to promote itself on the tourist map. As a tourist attraction, these spectacular restaurants may not be very demanding of the patron; they may not impose a strict dress code or require the patron to consume a formal meal, but instead will have an elegant dining area as well as ambient spaces outside the dining room where drinks and casual snacks can be purchased at relatively high prices.

There are also formal restaurants in this category that are celebrated as the finest examples of a particular culinary style with highly accomplished chefs, head-waiters and sommeliers. These restaurants create an atmosphere that adamantly repudiates the prosaic: some examples are The Four Seasons, The Russian Tearoom, Top of the Sixes in New York, La Tour d'Argent, Le Coq D'Or, Maxim's, Carré des Feuillants in Paris, Sukiyabashi Jiro, Ishikawa and Koju in Tokyo, Vue de Monde in Melbourne and Tetsuya's in Sydney, Gordon Ramsay's in London, and Chez Panisse and Ma Maison in California. The Four Seasons made its international reputation on its practice of altering its menu and decor with each change of season. As well as being a novelty, the practice allowed the restaurant to offer a wider variety of dishes. As a result, The Four Seasons has a well-established identity and regular patrons who have known the restaurant over its 50-year existence, and are familiar with its personnel and style. It also appeals to tourists who know about its corridor decoration, the Pablo Picasso stage curtain painted for Le Tricorne, as well as the Pool service, Grill Room and its popularity with world figures such as Henry Kissinger, Anna Wintour, Martha Stewart and Salman Rushdie. This all adds to the uniqueness of this otherwise architecturally ordinary restaurant. Thus, in many ways, The Four Seasons is the archetype of the formal spectacular *Fête Spéciale* that successfully combines celebrity and distinctive quality.

Yet the success of the *Fête Spéciale* is diminishing in the current climate of hyper-attention to cuisine and service. Its early confidence in developing style and extravagance as the hallmark of excellence has been eclipsed by a more knowing and worldly client. The six or seven decades of hegemony of the *Fête Spéciale* saw their fashionability rest on their elaborate presentations of *grande cuisine* with *pièces montées* freshly carved from pasta, butter or ice that were intended to over-awe the diner. Delmonico's in New York was a prime example as the home of extravagant dishes such as Lobster Newberg, Baked Alaska and the signature dish, the very thick-cut Delmonico steak. Food was served at the table with great ceremony; ornate vessels contained piquant sauces, the cutlery was abundant and there was a flurry of waiters who quickly presented the meal then retreated imperceptibly.

The original Delmonico's has faded away, but similar types of grand restaurants remain popular, especially when celebrating a special occasion such as a wedding. They are atmospheric and theatrical with deliberate effort made to suggest luxury and grandeur. Like a theater, the premises of some formal spectacular restaurants are transformed when they begin service from a plain structured room into a setting of seductive ambience. Their popularity is primarily the atmosphere and grandeur that evokes the memory of César Ritz's dining room at the Savoy Hotel, and the elaborate food carvings of the opulent and fashionable Delmonico's that dominated high society in the early twentieth century. The persistent dedication to presentation as a means of enchanting the diner is the chief characteristic. We choose these places for their luxury and excess: the more opulent, impressive and unusual they can appear, the stronger will be their reputation. In these restaurants, the symbolic encounter is not only with food but with the paraphernalia of aesthetic grandeur.

Half Moon is a formal spectacular restaurant located in the business district of a large metropolis. It occupies a low-rise Art Deco building that was once a private club. It is approached along a semi-circular drive that includes a porte-cochère; these are themselves signs of luxury in a city where space is expensive. The reputation of Half Moon rests with its celebrity chef who arrived in the country as an unskilled migrant twenty-five years ago and has since dedicated himself to the refinement of a French–Japanese fusion cuisine. Half Moon began as a local bistro in a suburban location surrounded by quotidian modesty. Over two decades, the reputation of the chef grew to such an extent that it supported relocation into the heart of the city along with a significant change of patronage. This change coincided with the financial boom of the 1990s. The clientele of the restaurant altered in stages from the adventurous diner looking for inexpensive novelty in the early days of the restaurant, to the fine dining of the banking fraternity, and now to the well-heeled tourist from Sydney or London knowing that dinner at a world-famous restaurant must be on the itinerary.

Half Moon has several separate rooms that surround an interior garden styled in traditional Oriental fashion. Large glass windows provide almost every table with a view to the outdoors. At night, the external lighting shapes the garden into a dark green background with sparkling white rocks and groomed pebble pathways. The stillness of the exterior is echoed inside the restaurant where dark wood wall panelling and thick grey carpet provide the soft background to well-spaced tables. After the fashion of the traditional Japanese restaurant, where diners have private rooms and do not encounter any other diners, Half Moon is internally designed to provide each table with utmost privacy. There are rooms where only one table is set, and other partial rooms that are carefully divided with smoked-glass panelling so diners are kept from seeing one another. For those occasional diners who wish to be seen and hope to spot a celebrity or two, the level of discretion is a hindrance, but to those brokering an important deal, perhaps a seduction or a commercial proposition, it is an advantage. Half Moon is effectively atmospheric: there is very little background noise and occasionally some minimalist music wafts through the rooms. Noise is important in creating ambience. It is not only noisy kitchens and clattering plates that supposedly interfere with a good meal, but also the loudness of other diners. Sometimes a small music combo or piped music may help to disguise unwanted noise; however, a certain level of buzz and bustle is necessary to evoke a feeling that we are at the center *à la mode*. At Half Moon, where the kitchen is concealed and the buzz is kept to a minimum, a sense of being at the center is not fully realized. This dining experience emphasizes the sensuous qualities of eating where the palate is being cultivated.

At Half Moon, the service staff are fresh-faced, impeccably well mannered and dressed homogeneously in simple dark clothes. The design of the restaurant is such that the diner cannot see where staff are stationed but the staff can see whenever a diner signals for service. A slight lift of the head, a searching glance over the shoulder, and very soon a waiter is at the table. The menu is simple and the wine list extensive. It is possible to request that the sommelier selects the wine to be served with each dish so the diner is relieved of any pressure to display knowledge of what would be appropriate. The meal is a continuous series of presentations; in between the primary courses, there are sample morsels served in aesthetically pleasing ways. These arrive at the table as unexpected diversions. The waiter suggests the diner experiment with this salmon slice or palate-cleansing shot-glass of clear soup. It is *dégustation* without being announced. The samples provide an opportunity for extended conversation with the staff as they explain why they have added these to the table. This also allows for conversation more generally about the menu, the garden and the celebrity of the chef. The staff are trained to expect this, and given the heart-warming story of the chef's rags to riches transformation, this moment of conversation is important as it allows the diner to experience a fleeting sense of control in the midst of this smoothly engineered experience. Half Moon provides a muted atmosphere that coddles the diner and sets the stage for the satisfaction of underlying pleasures one did not know existed.

All fine dining is expected to be an experience at a distance from the mundane. The mood generated by the restaurant is part of the purchase and can linger beyond the perimeters of the restaurant. Thus is dining transportive; it brings other social and cultural worlds to the table to supplant everyday habits. In this manner, Half Moon is a riposte to the prosaic. Its ambience is more than the décor and temperature of the restaurant; it is the ornament of mood that is nourished by the visceral sensations of new flavors and textures as well as the subdued density of the noiseless style. At Half Moon, we are immured in fashionable good taste; the plates, wine glasses and menu all exemplify an understated elegant stylishness; the dining experience meets Roland Barthes' admonition – to taste exotic fare in order to encounter the other. The staff are well trained and bring welcome explanations of the food to the table along with the aesthetically arranged meal on the dinner plate. We are gently taken into another sensuous domain where we are silently addressed through the elegance of the setting; that is, until we use the services.

A visit to the toilet brings a moment of sharp surprise. The two adjacent doors leading to the separated male and female toilets are adorned with a single, stark ornamental slice of burnished Florentine silver. This sculptured sign, no bigger than a human hand, is attached to the door at eye level and is so strange it requires a moment of focused interpretation. The vertical slash separating the male from female is represented with an obvious protuberance at each end, signifying breasts for the female toilet and a penis for the male. The sign is an instant reminder of the universal body and the natural processes of alimen-tation. The display of refinement and elegance in the dining rooms where food is transmogrified into aesthetic wonders is reduced at the doors to the separate toilets to a reminder of the stark biology of gendered plumbing. The use of the single, meaningful sign echoes the Chinese art of calligraphy that begins with the simplicity of the single line, usually horizontal rather than vertical as in this example, that eloquently separates, divides and hierarchically ranks the order of high from low, sky from earth, heaven from hell, night from day. At Half Moon, the question of which direction to take is forced into the consciousness of the diner standing in front of the subtly marked doors. The next question that arises in this moment of reflection is whether the visual reminder of the basic human body is a deliberate corrective to the exotic sensuous experience of the meal, whether as an amusing reminder that it is all an illusion, just froth and bubble; that no matter how we might strive to protect ourselves from the brutal reality of biology, it is irreducible; or whether this quirky and stylized sign is just a mistake, a lapse of taste in the otherwise elegant decor.

Some spectacular restaurants have a continuously changing clientele, mostly tourists who out of necessity do not usually press for gastronomically remarkable meals. People will dine at spectacular restaurants for their unique attractions and not always for the reputed cuisine. For example, the Shouting Restaurant in Tokyo originated as a spectacular restaurant that became famous not only for its cuisine but its manner of presentation. With its fame, however, and replication in London, New York, Singapore and Hong Kong, it has become a more casual restaurant. The diner still sits at a bench that encircles the cooking area and the food is still delivered on a long-handled wooden paddle. Conversation is restricted because of the noise generated by the practice of shouting the food orders. The meal is not taken over a leisurely few hours that, in some instances, offsets the high expense of dining out but is, instead, measured by the number of different courses consumed. The original attraction to the Shouting Restaurant was fashion, but over time, as this once unique restaurant has proliferated into a global chain, it has lost much of its fashionable allure. Reputation and fashion are both essential to the success of the spectacular restaurant. Indeed, these can impel the serious food adventurer to travel into rural areas for a Michelin star; for instance, at Sat Bains in Nottinghamshire, UK or Hôtel des Frères Troisgros in Roanne, France, with its celebrated kitchen that attracts visitors willing to observe the operations from a purpose-built viewing platform. To dine at Frères Troisgros or Sat Bains is to enjoy individually prepared dishes at high prices and to have the chef come to the table during the meal to enquire of one's satisfaction, and even to provide instructions on how best to eat the dish. Attention to detail is unsurpassed. Such dining experiences allow the claim that one is cultured and civilized. Cuisine may be important to an inveterate diner, but in these restaurants style has greater value. It attaches to the diner and thus demonstrates personal dedication to the very best that life presumably has to offer.

Engaging restaurants

This category is highly diverse, including restaurants that are expensive, oddly located, say, in a converted train carriage or refurbished factory, as well as positioned more conventionally on the high street where they are enjoyed as unpretentious neighborhood favorites. Their shared features include their accessibility not only in terms of physical location but also because of their inviting ambience. These are places for amusement and undemanding pleasure, although in the top-end *bistros mondain* there is an element of emulation of the spectacular restaurant. Thus they are so-named, using bowdlerised French, for their aspiration to haute cuisine and dedication to ambience that can verge on the imitative and pretentious.

The theme restaurant is one kind of bistro mondain that has enjoyed a variable history. In its early days (1970s to 80s), it provided a combined form of entertainment as a theater restaurant. As well as the meal, diners were involved in an interactive drama. It might be the case that the restaurant recreated a speakeasy from the American 1920s, and diners were instructed to use stock phrases like "The Godfather sent me" when making a reservation. The theatricality of these restaurants extends to include exchanges with the staff. If the restaurant resembled a Transylvanian grotto with waiters disguised as vampires and werewolves, the diner may be brought into a bantering exchange about the freshness of the steak and the life-enhancing qualities of the deeply red Sangria. The purpose of this is simply to provide amusement as well as overcome the unequal and always potentially difficult relationship between diners and restaurant staff. The attraction of the themed restaurant is its dramatic realization: it might be a floating pavilion moored at a riverbank decorated to appear like a remote tropical island or a dungeon grotto in a city back alley. More recently, the themed restaurant has been designed to appeal to children; for example, the M&M café at Leicester Square, London, which is a multi-storey candy shop that doubles as a café for kids; or the Rainforest restaurant where again the design and the menu are targeted at the child consumer.

In the themed restaurant, the decor has precedence. Diners can be entertained by the verisimilitude of the interior design and amused by the kitsch atmosphere. Such restaurants are popular with office parties or stag nights where the search for entertaining distractions is stronger than the interest in or desire for gustatory sensations. There are few regular patrons of such restaurants; they are better suited to group outings.

Dining out in a large group is more entertaining and successful here because the stylized environment creates cohesion. The parodic restaurant is suitable for groups where individuals may not know each other well. In this setting, any social awkwardness is minimized as the decor is so intrusive that it provides a focal point for conversation. Irrespective of the obvious inauthenticity of the themed restaurant, it is in some ways an honest form of dining insofar as its intentions to be entertaining and frivolous are explicit. In this restaurant, the creation of mood, the orchestration of the event and the engagement of the diner's imagination are the paramount features of the occasion, almost to the exclusion of the meal. Often the food is presented smorgasbord-style and lends itself to a colorful visual display but minimal variation in gastronomic tastes; dishes with subtle flavors that require rapid cooking and immediate serving cannot be presented in the economical style of the buffet.

The themed restaurant is part of the parodic category where the restaurant itself is the amusement with its fully recreated ethos and abundant novelties. In the parodic restaurant, be it a mock saloon of the nineteenth-century American wild west, a quaint English village tearoom, a Tuscan marketplace or tea clipper sailing ship, we expect the food to be less important than the setting. The enjoyment rests largely with the playfulness of the place; say, with its vast array of bric-a-brac on display and seemingly authentic furnishings and fittings.

The themed restaurant was very popular in the last quarter of the twentieth century. Hollywood had produced the Hard Rock Café in the late 1970s and has since generated more than a hundred spin-off outlets worldwide. Planet Hollywood opened in 1992. Originally, it operated as a consortium with dozens of celebrity film stars owning the iconic café. Dive!, the creation of Steven Spielberg, opened to a great fanfare in 1994. It offered gourmet sandwiches in tubular or submarine-shaped premises at Century City shopping mall (a mile from Rodeo Drive) in Los Angeles. The restaurant seated nearly 400 diners and spawned another outlet in Las Vegas. There were abundant visual gimmicks as part of the decor; fish and sea creatures moved about the ceiling, periscopes and circular windows gave a view onto other diners and the outside world; the menu featured clever puns and entertaining fare – sub-stantial salads and sub-lime desserts. There was also themed merchandise to buy including T-shirts, coffee mugs and carry bags. As entertaining and original as was the first Dive!, it did not capture a returning diner; it was a one-off experience and so in a matter of a few short years the business was in decline. The story of Dive! is common to other hyper-themed restaurants.

However, short-lived success is not the universal story; for instance, the McDonald's restaurant has been an ongoing global success. Its theme as a wholesome family restaurant for kids has always been less restrictive and definitive and thus its image has resisted becoming tired and unengaging. Also, the McDonald's business model uses highly engineered systems and processes that follow the Fordist principles of technology-driven mass manufacture, and these have ensured substantial profitability. The sustained global marketing campaigns have made the hamburger and fries into iconic products of America itself.

In his essays on hyperreality, Umberto Eco (1986) gives examples of reconstituted realities such as wax museums with their depictions of famous people and events, pleasure parks such as Disneyland and the extravagant decor of certain hotels, motels and restaurants such as those found in Las Vegas (Venturi 1977) to illustrate a peculiar feature of the modern consumer ethic; namely, an infatuation with the surface and appearances. The atmospheric bistro, designed to evoke a particular ethos, illustrates Eco's concept of hyperreality in which the present moment is constructed to lack depth. Some restaurants employ cultural mythology to recreate a setting based on popular images. The artefacts of the decor, the imitation pewter tankards and brass fittings, polymer brick walls, nylon fish nets hanging from the ceiling and so on have no claim to authenticity. They are absolute fakes (Eco 1986: 30–1), yet this attention to the manufacture of a particular mood and atmosphere has strong appeal. The parodic restaurant is an absolute fake, lacking even faithfully copied representations clearly marked as such that might give us an accurate idea of how the originals may have appeared, a style Eco describes as the "Almost Real" (1986: 30). The popularity of the parodic restaurant with its widespread use of absolute fakery represents an unambiguous disinterest with the real. It is a fabrication and this is its appeal.

Eco regards the pleasures found in the absolute fake as representative of a wider disinterest in recognizing the qualities of the reconstructed. We are not interested in the differences between the fake and the real; indeed, the fashionability of fake designer products such as Chanel handbags, Gucci watches and Hermès scarves has become valuable itself; it is a statement of disregard for the excesses of the consumer era. The idea that Eco presents is that the reproduction can be satisfying; as he states: "we are giving you the reproduction so you will no longer feel any need for the original" (1986: 19).

The stylish and themed restaurant shares some salient features with the more serious *bistro* insofar as all can be relatively expensive and dedicated to the management of the diner's imagination. However, there are striking differences that distinguish their patrons. Those who dine in the themed restaurant may not be habitual restaurant-goers and may more often see dining out as an occasion. With this diner, the heavily themed family restaurant such as McDonald's, Sizzler and Applebee's is also popular for its low cost and convenience. In its wide range of style and cuisine, the bistro mondain provides distinctive experiences and encourages a widely divergent repertoire of individual behaviors. In many instances, it strives for worldliness without being dismissive of local culture. The bistro is favored by those who value cuisine as a form of entertainment. It is popular for its use of decor to evoke a particular atmosphere such as a light open space for the health-conscious clientele of nouvelle cuisine or a darker-hued environment for those interested in the intimacy of dinner à deux. The bistro promotes cuisine and cost as its leading attractions, although a great deal of emphasis is also placed upon atmosphere. These restaurants are generally small, and the table service attempts to be personalized.

We might choose to dine in such a restaurant in order to feel in control of the situation and ensure we have our desires satisfied.

The fashionable locale of the bistro usually means it will be commercially successful even if it has only a limited menu and a dozen or so tables with some single seating at a communal table. It might be located near the theater district or a famous retail sector, say, for antiques and art galleries featuring emerging young artists. In some cases, it is more like a wine bar providing fussy but elegant light foods like lacquered pork with ginger confit, tuna tartar, select cheeses with chutney and bite-sized lobster claws. The style of the bistro is important: its table settings are *au courant*; it might use two tablecloths of complementary colors laid over each other diagonally, and cutlery that is heavy, highly polished, ornate and old-fashioned. The wine glasses may be extravagantly large and thin, almost too fashionable to be practical. In such a bistro, the diner wants to be seen and to see others. It is where we can look about and feel sure we recognize a face or two. Indeed, at the bistro we hope to meet our peers and encounter those whose tastes we want to mirror. It is a place we can also dine solo as it allows for bar service from attentive staff who treat us as knowledgeable about the wines, cheeses, olives, meats and other tapas that might be on offer. This recognition, that cultural capital has currency, means that the elegant bistro can be a reassuring haven for the confident diner.

In the highly acclaimed bistro that boasts locally sourced foods and a wine list featuring garagistes – the garage wines produced in exclusive small lots that sometimes attain enviable high quality – we recognize the importance of fashion. These idiosyncratic bistros were popular during the 1990s, but their reputations have paled somewhat since their concentration on style rather than substance has now been recognized as faddish. Nonetheless, it is their fashionability and success in securing a devoted diner that creates this category of dining. The bistro is the most familiar restaurant in that it has wide appeal, is well located in convenient places, and offers diversity in cuisine, ambience and cost. The popular series of eateries developed by David Chang is an example; beginning in 2004 with a quirky noodle bar, Momofuku Ko, in the East Village (New York) and then spinning off in the next five years to a small high-energy bar where securing a reservation was difficult and subsequently a key marketing technique. The *New York Times* food commentator, Frank Bruni (2008), described the restaurant as a site of "little tyrannies of discomfort" designed to emphasize the food rather than the decor. As Chang succeeds in spreading his culinary style to more widespread locations outside America, he runs the risk of making the Momofuku brand another Wagamama or Shouting Restaurant. The high profile achieved through television appearances, and the publication of recipes and food commentary, have made the restaurants extremely popular; but in the final analysis, Frank Bruni asks, are they "glossy snack bars" that derive their charm from being "raucous and rollicking" into the wee hours?

The bistro best serves two or four diners, and some restaurants emphasize this preference by offering items on the menu that are only prepared to be shared. The size of the tables is usually small so the seating of large groups poses logistical problems; indeed, it is not uncommon for group reservations to be refused. With large groups, the preparations of the chef and the presentation of the food are more difficult to coordinate, thus creating greater pressure on the kitchen. Also, such groups can be noisy and dominate a small restaurant, overpowering its ambience. The bistro is designed to elicit a mood that supports the pursuit of pleasure; it orchestrates our sensibilities and intensifies sensation. As such, it ritualizes the expression of emotions in public, making it a suitable site for sexual seductions, celebrations and complex transactions where personal investments are exposed and vulnerable. Dining out in the *bistro mondain* is not only a gastronomic event but also a performance of personal values.

The bistro can vary in size and character from a relatively intimate setting serving fewer than thirty people, to large establishments catering for 100 or more. It includes the moderately priced family restaurant and the expensive and comfortable cuisine-based bistro, as well as the fashionable and faddish. This is the restaurant most frequented by those who regard it as a regular feature of social life. The diner may have set habits and dine regularly at the local Sizzler and Applebee's or seek out culinary variety in the bistro that is positively reviewed by media commentators. The patrons of these bistros are also commonly the purchasers of wine books and gastronomic guides to the latest eating styles. Gourmandizing is a leisure pastime; learning the vocabulary of food and wine as well as acquiring the skills of the mezzaluna in the kitchen at home are all part of the pleasures of the regular bistro diner.

Some *bistros mondains* are entrepreneurial ventures that will succeed on reputation and fashionability, while others promote signature dishes of the celebrated chef. Restaurateurs are frequently challenged to meld sophisticated tastes with commercial efficiency. In some instances, the bistro seriously dedicated to gastronomy can be a commercial failure while having an enviable reputation. In other instances, the flexibility of this style of restaurant means it constantly reinvents itself to align with market trends. Their style and costs change in response to market trends and the emotional requirements of the diner. So, if we desire an evening of intimacy requiring a sense of seclusion, we can choose a bistro with booths rather than freestanding tables, subtle dim lighting, an open fireplace and a musician playing soft classical guitar. For a diverting evening where the restaurant supplies the entertainment, we can choose a specific cuisine where the preparation, presentation and manner of eating are the focus, such as a Korean restaurant where we sit on the floor and have the meal cooked at the table. If we are keen to impress our fellow diner, we might rely on the heavy baronial dignity of the bistro to create a suitable atmosphere. The appearance of the restaurant insinuates itself into our conduct and intermingles with the desires we have attached to the event. Its ambience, with its deliberately chosen furnishings, creates a particular mood. Inanimate objects that we view and handle become loquacious and define the physical space in ways that might mirror our own tastes. We consume the aesthetics of the restaurant as we do the food.

The *bistro mondain* is the type of restaurant well suited to the public management of human emotions and expectations. Unlike the fast food restaurant, which also trades heavily on diners' expectations, the *bistro mondain* sustains the orchestration over a lengthier period of time, and consequently its moral order is more complex and coherent; it enthrals us more effectively. The main attraction is not simply a place for the consumption of tasty or unusual or highly valued foodstuffs, it is also the arena in which we are prepared to enunciate desires that are not always evident in our everyday repertoire. The interplay between atmosphere and expectation allows the exercise of imagination and the opportunity to detach ourselves from the routines of everyday life.

Creating identity, atmosphere and ambience is a preoccupation of all restaurants, from the fast food outlet to those with Michelin stars. The early commentator on the restaurant, Jean Anthelme Brillat-Savarin, referred to this characteristic when he observed how restaurant patrons were somehow exaggerated in their behavior. It was as if the restaurant transformed people, allowing them to emphasize a single dimensionality of character; consequently they became the loving father bestowing fine foods upon his dependants, or an ardent lover capable of excluding the busy world in order to concentrate on the beloved, or the detached stranger alone in a new city who (confronting the existential chasm that supposedly surrounds us all and which is more easily concealed in the company of friends and family) assumes a level of intimacy that is not there and becomes the immediate friend to all – hail fellow well met. Such a diner acts as if the connections were deep and enduring (Brillat-Savarin 1970: 310).

Wolf is a fashionable new trattoria at the edge of the theater district. It is a converted shop, with a long narrow gallery with a full glass display window that allows passersby to look in. The dining area is at street level with tables of plain wood and no tablecloths that indicate the decor is less important than the food. There are large linen napkins and an open sea salt container on each tabletop. A small dish of cold-pressed virgin olive oil has replaced the pat of unsalted butter. At the front of the restaurant, a bar of well-upholstered high stools give diners a good view of the three chefs preparing the quick dishes in the galley kitchen. There is a brightly colored retro-designed meat slicer perched on the gleaming marble slab in the preparation area that evokes the European delicatessen of the early twentieth century. Being able to watch the chefs at work blurs a traditional boundary between the front and back areas, between, figuratively, the factory and the shop front. This collapse of separation has reduced the distance between the producer and consumer, and when this occurs it is for the express purpose of traducing the differences in social rank that separate the provender from the consumer.

In Wolf, the inversions and reversals of status and rank add to the experience; the chef is the artist, the diner a paying supplicant much like a museum visitor taking in the priceless art forms and cultural displays. Wolf is busy and noisy; not the restaurant for a slow romantic meal or serious conversation. The tables are close; a neighbor reaching above the general cacophony will be easily overheard. Reservations for a table in the evening are offered every hour and fifteen minutes; a table can have four covers per night. Wolf has a full kitchen on the lower floor along with another less popular dining area. The floors are polished; there are a few nondescript modern paintings on the walls – typically a vase of flowers, or a cut of meat with fruit. These are unremarkable and again underscore the disdain for decor where the emphasis, righteously claimed, is on the menu. Dishes are described in traditional terms and located in the area of Italy where they originate – Puglia, Trentino, Venezia, Roma, Sicilia – in order to educate the diner into the regional flavors of other climes. The offer is an authentic sampling of regional cuisine. Wolf was designed by a team of recent graduates from an elite university whose educational credentials, known to those who know but not overtly displayed, makes Wolf a leader of the pack; a genuine trattoria as understood by those who would know food and regional authenticity.

The Club is another bistro where the culinary arts are taken seriously and close attention is given to food as much as the atmosphere itself. In contrast to Wolf, patrons of The Club are required to meet a dress code; men are expected to wear a collar and tie and should they arrive without, they will be provided with the necessary item. The decor of the restaurant is fancy and delicate; the light fittings are Venetian glass, the wallpaper is embossed with an intricate pattern, there are massive gilt mirrors on the walls, the tablecloths are stiff and white. There are elaborate displays of glass and china ornaments that suggest aesthetic discernment and fine taste. It is as if each object was carefully selected for its intrinsic charm and value. The same care and percipience are seen in the preparation of the food where each morsel is delicate and crafted like the accompanying cut-glass goblets and Limoges plates. Every dish is individually prepared. The food is extensively handled; the chef sculpts the dish before it is delivered to the table. Some items on the menu require twenty-four-hour preparation and must be ordered when the table reservation is made. For those who do not know about the house specialty and order it from the menu, they will be informed if it is not available. A consequence of the disappointment may be to bring that diner back another time or it may be to impose more solidly the culture of the restaurant. This happens in other ways as well: at The Club, the diner does not instruct the waiter on how he would like a dish prepared, or request beef cooked medium not rare, or the hazelnut torte with ice cream not cream; rather the dish is accepted the way it is offered. If the diner makes a contrary suggestion, the waiter may politely reply: "I would be pleased if you would accept the way the chef prepares that particular dish for you." At The Club, the diner can respond pleasurably to the dishes presented, but alternate suggestions are not well received.

The diversity found in the category of engaging restaurants accounts for the enduring popularity and success of this dining venue. At one extreme is the global chain, McDonald's, which also reappears in the category of convenience restaurants given its ubiquity and apparent economy. At the other end of the spectrum are the more elegant and faddish restaurants that appeal to culinary trends and may have a more precarious commercial history, but which repeatedly gain the attention of the promiscuous diner who is continuously looking for novelty and pleasure.

Convenience restaurants

The final category is the convenience restaurant, so-called for its long hours of business, low-cost foodstuffs, neighborhood location and minimum demands on the diner. These restaurants range in variety from the small café and gastropub with its hybrid menu and a decor intended to be fashionable to the other end of the spectrum, the fast food chains – Denny's, Red Rooster, Hooters, Wimpy Bar, Kentucky Fried Chicken and the suburban restaurant that offers relatively low-cost foods. The outlets located on motorways at truck stops, airports and bus terminals can also be included in this category in addition to the food courts at shopping malls and suburban retail complexes. This category includes local specialist cafés serving Chinese, Mexican, Italian pizza, Greek, Turkish and others as well as the fast food chain restaurant. There is a hierarchy in this category based on reputation, ambience, service and expense; however, the distinctive feature of the convenience café is its economy. Even if some of these cafés dedicate effort to the creation of an atmosphere, it is ultimately the use of less costly ingredients that can be quickly prepared that characterize this type of restaurant.

At the close of the twentieth century in the UK, more convenience and fast food meals were consumed than any other. Of the two million plus commercial meals consumed in cafés and restaurants during 1998–9 (this excludes snacks), one million plus were identified as fast foods. These included pub meals, fish and chips, pizza and burgers, Chinese and Indian takeout (Burnett 2004: 291). In recent years there has been a

growing concern with the health risks of poor nutrition related to fast foods. International agencies associated with the OECD have collected data reporting the trends in obesity in countries with highly industrialized food systems. The UK, USA, Canada and Australia feature as the societies with the highest rates of obesity (http://www.oecd.org/health/health-systems/oecdhealth-data2012-frequentlyrequesteddata.htm). This data shows that women more than men and less educated women display higher rates of health issues related to being overweight. Sales of soft drinks have declined markedly over the past eight years, forcing manufacturers such as Coca-Cola, PepsiCo and Dr Pepper to diversify into sports drinks and fruit juices (Esterl 2013).

The ready availability of entertaining foods in affluent societies has created an expectation that dining out is an ordinary part of everyday life, and with the café mundane, this expectation is most often met. For instance, Piccoli is a gastropub located in a well-established suburb with a demographic mix of elderly residents and upwardly mobile young families. Most of the local inhabitants, both old and new, fit into professional and middle management occupations; they express a traditional leaning to the political right. Piccoli provides tables for families as well as smaller groups and couples. There is an open fireplace used during the winter months; the ceilings are high, in character with the period architecture of the building, and the lighting is strong but not bright. There are no tablecloths, flowers or candle centerpieces, and the crockery is simple white china. The napkins are a dark-colored heavy paper. The "specials" menu is a blackboard hung on a wall, and the table menu and wine lists are single sheets of computer-printed paper. A wide range of colorful pre-dinner cocktails is on offer. The prices are described as moderate. Patrons dine regularly at Piccoli as they know the menu and are confident that the quality of the food will be consistent. Reservations are not often required and there is little need to dress formally. Piccoli is casual and encourages family gatherings and social groups. There is piped music throughout that adds to the noise level. There is no rush to provide second covers on the tables. The table service is variable as the café personnel have a high turnover.

The decor at Piccoli creates a sense of nostalgia through clutter. On the walls are old movie posters, sepia photos of iconic cityscapes and streetscapes from New York and Paris that have the effect of producing a sense of famili-arity and comfort. Easily recognized images of Hollywood movie stars such as Marilyn Monroe, Steve McQueen and The Blues Brothers, and a heart-warming sepia photo of an Italian mama making bread in a wood-fired oven, portray the café as familiar, reassuring and welcoming (Hubbert 2007; Pardue 2007). In this type of restaurant, it is essential that a familiar atmosphere is created, as the common diner at these restaurants is not usually an adventurer but is seeking reassurance; the food is recogniz-able without esoteric menu descriptions and the service is unintimidating. Sometimes the decor and the food are not complementary; the café may create a bohemian ambience, or have potted palms that suggest the health and vigour of a tropical clime while the menu is simple; say, breakfast specials and lunches of soups, sandwiches, pasta and ready-made rice snacks. There may also be desserts such as apple pie, ice cream and commercially purchased profiteroles. Where the diner can confidently expect a certain gastronomic style from a glance at the decor of the fashionable bistro located in the upmarket sector of town, the café is not as self-revealing. Its decor may be incoherent and even clash with the foods on offer; it may look like a film set but serve basic meals with a limited range of choice. The physical appearance of the café mundane can be self-conscious; it may use rough-hewn wooden beams and new brass fittings to suggest an old-worldliness that in turn is supposedly evocative of an authentic regional cuisine. It may have stained-glass windows and a slate floor to suggest a Mediterranean flavor when its actual setting is the suburban outskirts. Yet for all its incoherence and variety of cuisine, the café mundane is very popular. It offers easy sociability and exposure to the possibility of engaging entertainment without the surprise of excitement.

In Quentin Tarantino's film, *Pulp Fiction*, there is a discussion of global foods between Jules, Brett and Vincent, the killer thugs, who find it remarkable that the McDonald's quarter pounder available in America is called a Royale with cheese when served in France. This brief exchange emphasizes the global nature of food tastes. Whether it is a cheeseburger in America or a Royale in Paris, the taste is the same. Inadvertently or not, the film scene is an advertisement for the McDonald's promise that its products will always be the same, always reliable, always meeting the expectations of its consumers no matter where they are served. The success of McDonald's chain restaurants has been extensively analyzed; from the shop that Mack and Dick McDonald opened in 1940 in San Bernardino, California to the ubiquitous golden arches that have appeared throughout the world under the corporate expansion engineered by Ray Kroc. The McDonald's marketing phenomenon has effectively changed the world of mass food consumption. Yet McDonald's, even with its robustly branded products, cannot always withstand local subversions that often reach a tipping point that change the product. This may account for the golden arches fading from McDonald's advertising as that image became more widely parodied as exaggerated hungry lips or, when inverted, a bulbous buttock.

The global success of the chain restaurant, and widely recognized products such as Coca-Cola, Pepsi and Bud, has been explained in theories of economic globalization, creolization and world systems with center-periphery tensions. These various accounts generally underscore the power of mass popularity and the effectiveness of saturation marketing principles. For example, the visually distinctive architecture of the American-based themed restaurant (including the maligned golden arches) and the iconic packaging of specific exported commodities such as Fosters beer, Marlboro cigarettes and Cadbury's chocolate are integral to consumer trends. When these commodities arrive in the exotic environment of the receiving society, whether India, the Philippines, Korea or Timor Leste, they are easily recognized. These products are marketed on a global scale and have successfully crossed cultural boundaries and breached the insularity of national and class identity in ways that other cultural products cannot. Convenience snacks and themed restaurants (such as the M&M café) have advanced the industrialization of food, thereby making their manufacturers and distributors, such as Nestlé, Mars, Cadbury's and Unilever, into some of the world's largest and most politically influential corporations (Nestle 2002).

In the twenty-first century, more than 90 percent of the American public has eaten at McDonald's. There are thousands of outlets across the globe. To meet the constant changes of consumer tastes, the original offer of the hamburger and fries has also changed without appearing to do so. McDonald's restaurants now dispense soy and lentil burgers, salads, sweet fruit pastries and cappuccinos while still ensuring that its original successful product remains. Wherever the hamburger is sourced, whether in Greenwich Village, Piccadilly Circus, the Champs-Élysées or Milan's Duomo Arcade, the reliability of pleasure is assured. This assurance, more than the food itself, is the ingredient for success. Convenience foods are sold on the basis of continuity. In a fast-moving world where much is unpredictable and where life patterns can be discontinuous and transient, the promise of stability, of providing a "home away from home" found in familiar tastes, has proved highly successful. Even though the McDonald's promise states that it will always be the same, in actuality, local tastes are incorporated in response to market demand. Grits have been added to the breakfast menu in some southern states of the USA and croissants in some European outlets. It is not these idiosyncratic responses, however, that ensure the success of McDonald's but the promise that the burger and fries will always be the same. These are the signs of stability and reliability in a world that to some can seem too fluid.

SERVICE AND STYLE

Much of the pleasure of dining out rests on managing the social tensions inside the restaurant. The food may be outstanding, and the comfort of the restaurant assured, but these pleasures can be diluted when the service is unexpectedly slow, the waiter insouciant and the decor unnecessarily intrusive. Some restaurants pay close attention to the conduct of the staff on the understanding that much of the pleasure of dining lies in its emotional tenor. Maximizing these pleasures often involves managing the waiter. A method of ensuring quality service is to androgynize the staff; similar dress codes for males and females symbolically demonstrate that gender is being subsumed and that the diner – whether male or female – will be treated equally. Such practices tacitly recognize the importance of service, knowing that it can become awkward and take an unexpected turn; then the event can lose its gloss and the illusions created by its performative nature will be exposed.

At the same time, the restaurant borrows from the wider society and can use status and gender differences to its commercial advantage. In the theme restaurant, Hooters, for instance, originating in the southern states of the USA and now expanding into the UK and Asia, there is an overtly sexualized atmosphere. The waiters are young nubile women who serve mostly male diners interested in food that is simple and beer that is cold. The women are dressed as American high school cheerleaders who might be just as comfortable urging their sports team to ever-greater heights as they are waiting on tables. They generate a slightly raunchy tone that echoes a stereotyped depiction of relations between the sexes.

At the most obvious level in any restaurant, there is a divide between the provider and consumer; however, this is not an equal divide. The chef/restaurateur, the waiter/server and the diner/customer each represent different sets of interest that share a shifting structure. The chef and waiter often work as a team, but they can also be in opposition to one another. The diner and waiter can form an alliance in which the waiter provides insider information that benefits the diner and, at another time, the waiter may exploit the diner in order to meet other interests.

Providing service in a modern liberal society normalizes inequalities created by commercial and social instruments such as money, gender, age and status. As with most service relationships, the consumer expects that the purchased service will be direct, utilitarian and efficient, and this is presumably assured by the commercialism of the exchange. The attractive simplicity of the calculated commercial exchange is that any inherent inequality between the parties is understood and accommodated; that is its primary benefit. However, the mediation of money does not always ensure this equality. When these transactional rules are overlaid with emotions, when the exchange is charged with unexpected displays of indifference, overt familiarity, sexual innuendo or resistance of various kinds, then the reductive and simplifying capacity of the monetary system is inadequate. The restaurant provides ample opportunity for social complexity as its overt purpose is to deliver pleasure and satisfy desire; embedded in the event are expectations that other appetites – along with the gustatory – will be satisfied. In these ways, the emotional and sexualized atmosphere of the restaurant can further emphasize the emotional exposure and vulnerability of the diner, especially in fine dining, where the explicit purchase of human service is part of the pleasure.

When Georg Simmel (1858–1918) considered the question of how society is possible, he focused on the minimalist social interaction between two (the dyad) and then three parties (the triad). It was, he argued, a perspective that explained the domestic as well as the institutional. Small and large-scale institutions develop from the same basis, so that the principles of exchange observed in close interactions are repeated and amplified on an ever-increasing scale to support larger organizations. Societies can thus be explained from the bottom up. The restaurant provides a vivid illustration of these fundamentals of sociality; it is a stage setting for dyadic and triadic formations and thus illustrates how the objective culture of the external social world penetrates into the subjective dimension of human congress and becomes part of the vocabulary of personal identity.

Simmel regarded the dyad as the basic and most readily understood social building block. Here the two parties or individuals are in direct communication; their exchanges produce the necessary social cohesion that keeps them together. Power is equally shared as both have the same opportunities to remain face to face or turn away and dissolve the situation. With the introduction of a third person or party, the dualistic exchange becomes more complex and unpredictable. In the dyad, the most basic of all exchanges, the power distribution flows back and forth between the two parties and there is very little capacity for one to assume greater influence over the other. The triangle or triad is the more common formation in everyday social life, and it presents a complex situation in which tensions and unpredictable exchanges of power take place, thereby making every social encounter a situation that needs to be controlled.

In the triad, the appearance of a third point creates opportunities for re-alignment and a competitive struggle for primacy. It reveals the fluidity of situations and how marginal interests can in certain instances become dominant and vice versa. The triangle creates both super and subordinate positions, and introduces the radical dynamics of the master-slave relationship. By definition, all triadic exchanges involve dissent, tension and a struggle for dominance; as such, they create a need for arbitration and provide the third party with the opportunity to act as powerful broker. The *third member* can negotiate the social balance, and with that position comes extra benefits. This position is also known as the laughing third party as it can take advantage from the tensions between the others. It can offer to mediate in a non-partisan way or display a preference for one position over the other two. The third party gains advantage by appearing to offer benefits to each. This jockeying for power and influence can twist into other formations if two parties join forces and oppose the third, thus establishing a dyadic relationship, and this makes all others irrelevant. The dyad and triad dominate the internal culture of the restaurant and continually influence its emotional tempo as they shift and re-establish themselves during the event.

To be the third point in the triad is to exert the greatest influence. At one point, the waiter may mediate between the chef and the diner. In another posture, the waiter may act against the interests of the chef and recommend to the diner a dish that is better on the day than another. A further advantage can be taken by waiters who act entirely for their own benefit against the interests of both the chef and diner, as in the instance where "fiddles" are executed, described by Nicod and Mars (1984). The power of the waiter has also been described in terms of choreography and space management (Erickson 2007); at their discretion, they allocate territory and prescribe the amount of movement of individuals inside the restaurant. The diner is directed to a table by the waiter, and not all tables provide the same experience; some are noisier than others, they are nearer to the kitchen, or toilets, or front door and passageways, and this can impinge on the dining experience. The waiter's body language can frame the diner's experience and create a sense of intimacy as when the waiter introduces themselves and offers to be of help, which has become more common in the casual bistro:

"Hi, I'm Scott, and I'll be your server for the evening." Alternatively, the waiter can be remote, formal, or even distracted, and this in turn conveys the message that the diner is not very important.

The chef too has the opportunity to act in the position of the third point in relation to other restaurant staff and the paying customer. In the former instance, the chef can be a diva and act with aggressive superiority towards the kitchen staff. Such posturing is justified by a chef who is aligned with the paying customer and is motivated to provide excellence, even if this means taking an oppositional attitude towards restaurant staff. In this instance, the chef may be over-concerned with the perfection of the preparation and make every dish that leaves the kitchen into a signature work of art. This dedication to the culinary arts positions the chef at the pinnacle of the triangle, as the point of focus for both the diner and staff alike. The chef's deep attachment to food elevates his position to that of master. Such dedication was exemplified by Jiro Ono of the three Michelin-starred restaurant in Tokyo, who treated his body as if it were a direct element in determining the olfactory sensations of his diners; and Sat Bains of the Michelin-starred restaurant of the same name in the Midlands, UK, who regularly tramps the local fields and market gardens in search of the best local ingredients to offer his diners; and Odessa Piper of L'Etoile in Madison, Wisconsin, who similarly champions local ingredients as a means to improve the American palate (Trubek 2007: 35–43). This dedication to food places the chef in an expert superior position, and provides a reason for their wariness of the diner who probably knows very little about the dishes being prepared and the subtleties of their flavor, color and texture. As the role of chef has become increasingly professionalized and celebrated, the disjuncture between their skills and their reception by their audience creates another kind of struggle in the realization of self-interests. Amy Trubek (2007: 35) asks: "why are some chefs championing their knowledge of ingredients at the same time that almost all consumers know less and less about where their food comes from?" The chef in this instance can become the least appreciated participant in the dining experience. Their highly developed skills and years of strenuous training are irrelevant to their clients who have insufficient knowledge about food to be fully appreciative. The chef can be the authoritarian artist who emphasizes the superiority of haute cuisine as well as the anonymous functionary in the industrialization of the food system who, if employed by a mass food manufacturer or fast food chain, is an assistant in the promulgation of culinary homogenization and the uniformity of consumer experiences.

The triangular configurations in the restaurant influence the tenor of dining out. When the restaurateur/chef and the waiter are aligned together, as is most often the case, the diner becomes the third point of the structure that provides their mutual focus. The chef and waiter work together to influence the diner in their choices from the menu, and in the amount of money they may spend. The diner appears to be the *raison d'être* for the other two. The diner requests certain foods and is ultimately satisfied or not with the meal. Before the era of social media communication, the diner's best response was the size of the tip or gratuity added to the final bill. Now, with blogging and YouTube, diners have acquired the power of opinion to affect the reputation and even success of the restaurant. Consumers can easily comment on their experiences in hotels, restaurants, airlines, department stores and so on. The influence of these discourses remains variable. Inside the restaurant, however, the three positions of the waiter, chef and diner are engaged in an immediate dynamic of constant movement and adjustment. The angling and grinding of the positions gives the event a fluid nature in which the general structural features of all small-scale interactions of everyday life (not just those of the restaurant) are played out, and in this sense the experience of dining out contains the essentials of every social experience.

FOOD AS NARRATIVE

We often look for a sense of excitement and self-enhancement by dining out, as we change daily routines and publicly exert ourselves through this act of conspicuous consumption. In the confined space of the restaurant, we are variously exposed to the close proximity of others. As we pursue our own pleasures, we are at the same time being observed, or think we are. The reactions of others to us, as well as their own expressions of exuberance and pleasure as they pursue their pleasures, combine to make the restaurant an environment in which modes of behavior must necessarily be subtly managed and disciplined. When dining takes place over several hours, we are more exposed to the vagaries of the situation, and thus the tempo of the restaurant needs to have in-built mechanisms that cordon off the performances of each table from the next.

To analyze dining out through the direct interests of the players brings attention to the different personal investments that are involved. How individuals act in the restaurant (irrespective of its type) is shaped by well-known conventions and practices. Within this frame, as we interact with one another we exercise a creative consciousness through which our own interests are realized. These claims for personal pleasures are less private than we imagine, as they commonly chime with the economic practices in current circulation. At this point, the objective culture of public actions is indistinguishable from the repertoire of subjective goals. The continuous movement between the internal and external stabilizes the fluid social context into a recognizable sense of shared reality. The private and public are inseparable, and the personal pursuit of pleasure, such as in dining out, regulates broader ideals of personal pleasure, happiness, a sense of virtue and success.

When we knowingly purchase the culinary skills of the chef and the presentational excellence of the serving staff, we are aware that from the moment of entry into the restaurant we are engaged in a highly mannered event. From the beginning until *le quart d'heure de Rabelais*, when the bill is settled, we are united with the restaurateur, chef and waiter in the conjuring of our own pleasure. The emotional intensity can in some circumstances enhance the meal and in other circumstances redeem a meal of disappointing fare. Good service does not always correspond with good food, although presentation has become so important that it can redirect attention away from the food and the conduct of the staff. In some restaurants where the spectacular setting and reputation of the chef are prominent, the temper of the waiters can be largely irrelevant. Ambience and decor are often promoted in commentaries on dining out on the assumption that a well-constructed atmosphere matches the quality of the cuisine. Comments on the waiter are less frequent; more attention is paid to abstract ideas such as celebrity, fashion, aesthetics and the popularity of new tastes such as regional cuisine and its authenticity, locality and veracity (Paules 1991; Fine 1996).

Barthes (1982) suggested that unless we take the opportunity to reflect on broader cultural issues when savoring exotic fare, we are avoiding the significance of the restaurant as a glossary of culture. If we follow Barthes' injunction, and take food as an invitation to enter another culture, we expand the possibilities for our own emotional pleasure: the encounter with food – in any setting – is an encounter with a symbolic system. The color, texture and shape of the food, the place where it is purchased, who has prepared it and where it is consumed all shape its significance and meaning. In her famous essay "Deciphering a Meal", Mary Douglas (1972: 61) pointed out: "if food is treated as a code, the messages it encodes will be found in the pattern of social relations being expressed. The message is about different degrees of hierarchy, inclusion and exclusion, boundaries and transactions across the boundaries". The respective ideas of Barthes and Douglas impel us to look at contemporary practices of food consumption as a means of understanding the emotional undercurrents of society. As mundane as eating is, and as regimented as dining out can be, nonetheless, in the style, preparation and nature of the food there are engaging cultural and symbolic dimensions that make it more than it seems. To dine on different foods introduces us to a new mentality and cultural arrangement of ideas, and the effect of this can be to highlight some basic assumptions of social life. As we savor the recreated dishes of old Europe through regional cooking and *cuisine terroir*, as we unwrap the skilfully fan-shaped napkin in the Japanese restaurant, and observe the re-emerging patterns in the porcelain of the Chinese bowls as the contents are slowly consumed, we are offered an invitation to explore another cultural universe.

At the same time, it must not be overlooked that food is big business and restaurants are themselves an important segment of the food economy. In London, at the turn of the twentieth century, there was a bull market in the restaurant trade as the celebrity of chefs entered its glorious decade. Estimates of its value to the national economy measured in the billions of pounds (*The Independent*, 8 September, 1998). In Manhattan, Sydney and Manchester, the story was the same; new restaurants opened regularly. After a decade or two, even the most celebrated and successful began struggling; the close of Stephanie's in Melbourne was a startling event. This haute cuisine restaurant moved into a gracious historic mansion in 1981 with its serious and generous chef, Stephanie Alexander, and closed in 1997, after which she turned to writing (Alexander 2002; 2012). Twenty years with a successful business is not a failure, but this event marked the realization of the downward turn in high-end dining. Another sign was the closing of the fine dining restaurant in Sydney's exclusive hotel, the Ritz Carlton, after only a year in business (Ripe 1993: 132). The rejection of formality in dining seemed to be the cause more than the high cost; there was greater enthusiasm for the bistro – the smaller, more atmospheric restaurant that provided for a few dozen diners rather than a hundred, and offered authentic dishes, or seemingly so, without much extravagance.

The trend is seen in the writing on restaurants, which itself has become an industry. Every large metropolitan daily newspaper devotes some space to commentary on eating, food styles, restaurants and celebrity chefs. How this commentary supports the restaurant business is difficult to gauge, as is the influence of the commentators. Critical writing about daily life has a respectable history (viz. the diaries of Pepys and Samuel Johnson); however, when it is focused on a particular industry such as the entertainment industries, there is a question as to whether this type of journalism is intended to have an impact on public opinion. Is the role of the food commentator to be a taste-maker in the sense of prescribing to others what they should and should not like?

When John Walsh, for instance, writes in *The Independent* that a restaurant's menu is unambitious or that it makes claims beyond belief – such as the chips being always triple-cooked, and the salted honeycomb in the pudding, despite all appearances to the contrary, appears as an unwrapped candy bar that can be purchased at the local grocery – the reader might be amused and might also be warned that that particular restaurant may not be worth the cost (6 October 2012, *The Independent*). When A.A. Gill writes that the recently published *Michelin Guide 2013* is bloated and unconvincing (*Vanity Fair*, November 2012), and when the writers at the *Observer* and *Guardian* newspapers, Elizabeth Day and Matthew Fort, respectively, comment on the success of a middle-range UK chain restaurant with a pretentious French name extending its market to France, where it aims to capture the same lower-middle-class diner who seeks a variety of taste but without the high price tag ("Should we worry about the rise and rise of Pret?", 8 April 2012), are we to take their views at face value? Presumably the point of such commentary is to encourage chattering in the public domain, which is a valuable feature of a demotic society but, when all the chattering is said and done, where is the authoritative base of the opinion?

While the discourse around food as provided through the mass media sustains a popular view that restaurants and dining out are essentially forms of entertainment, there is a more serious side to the business; namely, the influence of the agri-food corporations. Clapp (2012), Nestle (2002) and many others have argued that the influence on food habits and patterns of consumption exerted by global food businesses is much greater and more consequential than any amusing, critical or enthusiastic commentaries found in local newspapers or the social media blogging sites where both contented and disgruntled diners share their views. The public debates on genetic modification of foods, health issues and trade practices have been dominated by the interests of the agriculture and biotechnology companies, with the consequence that our general knowledge about the quality and value of food has become more removed and we are less able to evaluate the claims made by food manufacturers and retailers (Clapp 2012: 121). The recent scandal in the UK and Europe where horsemeat was introduced into beef products illustrates the problems with highly industrialized food retail, where the supply chain is so long it provides opportunities for the unregulated incorporation of extraneous materials.

In the process of fashioning appetite, there are myriad influences that exert themselves directly on our sensations and perceptions as well as on the material products we encounter in the supermarkets and in the cafés and restaurants of our choosing. The restaurant is a theater and according to an experienced restaurateur, the elements that ensure its success are food that is consistent, interesting but not challenging; comfortable furniture; soft lighting; clean uniforms on the staff; and courteous, unobtrusive service (Ripe 1993: 131). Such commentary may be an accurate description of some part of the experience, but it under estimates the influence of the desires of the diner who consciously or not relocates their private interests into the public domain whenever they choose to dine out.

When we act in the social world in the belief that we are knowledgeable consumers, demonstrating autonomy and independence, we generally set aside the more abstract influences that play over us from the local culture and historical circumstances. As a result, the sense of autonomy we experience derives from seeing ourselves as having floating identities that adapt to the immediate environment. Thus we arrive at a position of knowing we are shaped by concerted external influences, yet we feel confident in assessing the autonomy of our own performance. We are capable of having a pleasant meal as well as writing on the next available blogging site that we did not. We consider ourselves active agents, capable of managing the circumstances in which we live. By looking closely at elements of the everyday, such as the banal practice of dining out, we can identify specific challenges to this position. For instance, when taking pleasure in the public arena, before an audience of strangers, we tacitly observe conventions and prescriptions that ensure easy sociability and conformity. If we throw food on the floor, take morsels from the plates of other people, or spit out food we do not like, we are violating the rules of the situation if not actual legal standards of public health. To enjoy dining out, we must insert ourselves into the heavily engineered space that is the restaurant. Even the casual atmospheres of Hooters, McDonald's and Sizzler have overarching regimes that define the experience; these influences are also at play in the more elaborate, fashionable and expensive restaurants where we might imagine we have greater agency. Dining out in all its variety produces questions about the dimensions of our personal agency, and about what we think of as pleasurable and important to our sense of identity. By reviewing ordinary eating habits such as dining out, we are made more aware of the extent of the external cultural influences that inform our personal values, and in turn we are provoked to reconsider the extent of our agency.

4   MICHELIN STARS AND WESTERN OBESITY

There has been an explosion of interest in food. Primetime television has distinguished chefs such as Graham Kerr, Kylie Kwong, Nigella Lawson, Michel Roux, Nigel Slater, Jamie Oliver, Gordon Ramsay, Rick Stein and many more, all in their various indoor and outdoor kitchens demonstrating the best ways to prepare and present every conceivable dish in their repertoire. Metropolitan newspapers regularly include sections on gourmet dining and reviews of restaurants that range in timbre from reportage on a new opening or recent closing, to hyperbolic critique and enthusiasm by a foodie journalist intent on influencing public opinion (see the *Guardian*; *The Age*; *Sydney Morning Herald*; *New York Times*). There are also documentary films showing the internal workings of the busy kitchen in a five-star hotel, a celebrity chef cultivating boutique wine in a privately owned French vineyard, global food conglomerates testing hybrid grains that have been bioengineered in industrial laboratories, and the escalating trends in the incidence of diabetes and obesity that are in turn creating health panics in the industrialized West. Entertaining cinema has used food to focus a narrative, e.g. *Babette's Feast* (1987), *Chocolat* (2000), *Tampopo* (1985), *The Cook, the Thief, his Wife & Her Lover* (1989). Such attention shows the amount of interest and hyperbole surrounding food and how prominent it has become as a social spectacle.

Against such a background, the Michelin-starred restaurant and the obese body are both familiar images that appear in the mass media and represent two radically different depictions of human consumption. Eating is intimately involved with the body. Whether it takes place in a celebrated restaurant or in the privacy of the home, food has cultural importance that taps into a variety of dramatically divergent value systems. Eating fine foods prepared by an artisan chef in a restaurant of considerable reputation is supposedly one of the great sensory pleasures of the cosmopolitan world. It is an experience that is esteemed within a culture where cultivated tastes represent aspirations for the status-conscious. At the same time, there are numerous reports that show obesity is increasing at alarmingly high levels and that the over-indulged body (estimated to be one in ten adults) represents an epidemic of uncontrolled consumption (http://www.thelancet.com/journals/lancet/article/PIIS0140-6736(10)62037-5/abstract).

Changes in consumer patterns can in part be related to the practices of the food industries. For instance, in a short five-year span, the annual global sales of the top ten food retailers grew by 50 percent, while in the same time period the top ten food manufacturers grew by only 7 percent (Rabobank 2000). It would appear, from such reports, that we are being heavily influenced in our purchasing habits by the marketing techniques of retailers and advertisers more than by the availability of products. These reports also underscore the high activity of the advertising media in shaping consumer habits. In response to this trend, the Department for Environment, Food and Rural Affairs (DEFRA) in the UK reported on the need for a new food strategy that recognized the dominance of the retailer, and recommended a corrective approach that rebalanced the power relations between farmers, suppliers and big retailers to ensure the consumer had more choice, and that the growing trends of high consumption of junk foods were reduced (Lawrence, the *Guardian*, 5 January 2010).

In a society where consumer tastes are well developed, the obese body represents a failure to resist temptation. It suggests a capitulation to external coercions such as the onslaught of manipulative advertising. As such, the obese body becomes a reviled object. This is ironic as food itself has become an important focus for cultural and commercial activity and is constantly offered as a symbol of status and success. Food production and consumption is at the center of a global economy that drives the contemporary consumer culture; it influences the type of popular entertainment delivered through the mass media via advertising and capital investment, and as such it directly and indirectly affects individual preferences for leisure and pleasure. In such a context, the links between fine dining in a Michelin-starred restaurant and the increasing levels of obesity in the West rest on the constant attention paid to food, to its visual and hyperbolic representation in images that unequivocally privilege food in all its variety – from a candy snack bar to cooking programs on global broadcast television.

THE PERFECT MEAL

When the Tokyo-based restaurant Sukiyabashi Jiro received the endorsement of three Michelin stars, it was a surprise to the gourmandizing audience who had been habituated to the excellence of French cuisine ever since the Michelin guides gained their status. Sukiyabashi Jiro broke new ground in the reputation of the *Fête Spéciale*. The restaurant is small, with little attention paid to an aesthetic decor.

It is an undecorated, almost clinical space not located in an exquisite setting but in a basement near a train station in the busy heart of Tokyo. The choice to bestow three stars on this apparently modest establishment may have a great deal to do with the history of the Michelin system as well as with the shifting consumer interest in quality foods that lack the heavy additives of tradition. Tokyo now has more Michelin three-star restaurants than Paris, and it also has hundreds of restaurants with one or two Michelin stars. The massive population in Tokyo compared to smaller European cities means there is a greater number of restaurants competing to capture diners with shifting tastes in food styles, and this produces competitive high standards.

In Sukiyabashi Jiro, the diner is presented with the food and little else, apart from the unique experience of being almost hand-fed by the attentive chef. There are no accessories on the table, no wasabi, no soy sauce to add to the taste and no utensils. The food is presented in a traditional style and the diner eats with their fingers. First, a taste of *karei* or flatfish, then squid, *katsuo* or seared tuna, *uni* or sea urchin and *tamago* or egg. The sequence appears to follow a civilizing logic from the most cultivated and sophisticated tastes down to the most basic and natural.

The chef, Jiro Ono, paces the meal according to the speed with which his guests eat. Jiro Ono and his son have attained celebrity status for the purity of their food and the meticulous dedication shown to its preparation. Jiro Ono has been making sushi for more than seven decades and has concentrated on perfecting its presentation and taste. To this end, he has groomed his body, especially his hands, as the instruments for reaching this perfection. He claims to have worn gloves for the past fifty years whenever he is outside in order to protect his skin, and to have refrained from eating onion or garlic, smoking cigarettes, and drinking coffee and alcohol in order to ensure his skin does not transfer any tastes or aromas that contaminate the food and interfere with the diner's culinary enjoyment. His body itself is a utensil for cooking.

The competition for the Michelin star endorsement has been closely tied to the changing habits of the new middle classes of early twentieth-century Europe. The story begins with the interest in touring and the popularity of the motor car at the beginning of the twentieth century. It is also colored by nationalistic fervor as segments of the French bourgeoisie organized themselves into social networks to encourage tourism throughout regional France in an effort to assist in the country's economic growth. An association such as the Touring Club of France, founded in 1890, was operated in order to build a better international tourist trade (Young 2002). Part of their activities was to support the growth of French *terroir*, the authentic agricultural produce of Republican France.

The idea of discovering the authentic has been key to understanding the growth of tourism on a global scale during the twentieth century, and it has complemented the search for personal identity and status for members of the socially mobile affluent middle classes (MacCannell 1989). While the name Michelin is readily associated with food and high-quality restaurants, in its original incarnation it was (and remains) a tire manufacturer. The company quickly recognized the benefits of linking car travel and food tourism; from its early days, it included recommendations about the quality of the food, hotel accommodation and rural scenery to be encountered while traveling through France (Harp 2002: 23–5).

The growth of the company is also linked with nationalism and the commencement of the Tour de France bicycle race in 1903. By the 1930s, the company was engaged with promoting both tourism and French cuisine. It developed its now globally recognized icon Bibendum (the Michelin Man) in a prescient marketing gesture that has remained effective into the present era. It is an odd image for food, yet has proved enduring: the name of the portly Bibendum, from the Latin *nunc est bibendum* (now is the time to drink), could be argued to represent consumption, to drink in air, to cover distance, to go forward – all suggestive of movement and progress. In its earliest incarnations, Bibendum sported an upper-class image, sometimes carrying a walking cane, and wearing pince-nez and decorative rings on fingers that were clasped around the stem of a champagne glass. The representation has passed through stages; once a much more avuncular figure with spare tires of girth that gave an endorsement of sorts (intentional or not) to the pleasures of excessive consumption and, more recently, slimmed down with broader shoulders and a much more athletic silhouette. These changes to Bidendum's body and silhouette mirror the changes in physical appearance that we now associate with social success.

The zenith of the Michelin star system appears to have been reached at the end of the twentieth century and has waned slightly, at least in Europe. A number of investigative reports on the internal workings of the company have been published, and the previous secrecy around the practices of the Michelin inspectors has long been breached. Doubts have been in circulation about the reliability of the evaluation process; there are now too few inspectors making too few visits to give an up-to-date and accurate account of a restaurant's standard. Of more importance, perhaps, has been the growing degree of disgruntlement among the top restaurateurs who had previously been slavishly pursuing the Michelin endorsement. In addition to maintaining excellence in haute cuisine, the three-star award also required exceptional standards of presentation in the dining room with high-quality china and cutlery, elegant crystal glasses, luxurious linen, an abundance of fresh flowers on display, even including expensive art works on the walls. These associated costs with preening the decor of the Michelin-starred restaurant were beginning to seem disproportionate to the rewards of being so recognized. When a few celebrity chefs (Nico Ladenis, Marco Pierre White, Alain Senderens) refused the three-star Michelin award on the basis that the burden of recognition and maintaining a sparkling dining room did not necessarily make the food taste any better, the allure of the system was critically weakened. This trend followed closely from the much-publicized suicide in 2003 of Bernard Loiseau, chef at La Côte d'Or in the Burgundy region of France. This event was associated, rightly or wrongly, with the psychological and financial stress of achieving and maintaining the status of a Michelin three-star restaurant.

Aside from the secrecy and scandals associated with the dominance of the Michelin star system, the interesting aspect of this hegemony is the influence it exerted over food tastes and fine dining for more than half a century. The Michelin era summarizes the modern transformation of food into an imaginary experience based in the various processes of industrialization that have shaped the twentieth century. The incongruity of the Michelin icon, an anthropomorphized vertical tube of rubber tires in association with the glamorization of the culinary arts, remains puzzling. Trends in fine dining have changed, moving away from the superiority of classical haute cuisine that was worth an expedition through the regional areas of France, to a more innovative, new age cuisine that adopts regional and ethnic flavors without the formality, grandeur and posturing of an old world style.

The food writers M.F.K. Fisher, Julia Child and Waverley Root did much to promulgate the reputation of French cuisine; however, the elevation of food as a sign of human sophistication does not rest with a single culinary style. Food preparation is so diverse that it is valued now more readily for its commitment to experimentation. For instance, in the early period of the restaurant's global popularity, culinary innovations such as Brazilian churrascaria, Japanese miso ramen, Korean umami and Umbrian salumi had limited appeal and were not destined then to become global tastes, unlike the remarkable hegemony enjoyed by French cuisine. By the late twentieth century and into the twenty-first, new tastes and presentation styles were sought, and the search for signs of originality that re-frame cooking as a new form of art has become the prevailing interest. For instance, the introduction of *nouvelle*.

Nouvelle cuisine in the 1970s brought a schismatic change in the perception of food with its thin, almost transparent, slices of meat, its oversized plates that contrasted with the delicate fragility of the bite-sized morsel, and the soaring restaurant bills that soon brought about its own demise. Despite the *schadenfreude* that followed this fashion, nouvelle cuisine did signal a long-lasting shift in the estimation of food. Bourdieu (1984) recognized such changes as being an effect of social mobility. As we move up the social scale and acquire different aesthetic values and cultural capital, we are more interested in light, nourishing foods and a diet that maintains a slender, toned body. Hence the rich casserole was replaced by the multi-colored salad niçoise and the delicately prepared sushi.

Nouvelle cuisine was so enthusiastically embraced by the adventurous diner that it took some time before the reality of too little on the plate for too much cost was gently spoofed, then ridiculed and finally set aside as commercially unsustainable. Nouvelle cuisine had been too quickly exploited by the canny restaurateur who saw profit above value. In its defence, nouvelle cuisine was experimental and used the best ingredients. It was labor-intensive, thereby more expensive, but it was also highly aesthetic, simple (but not simplistic), fresh and healthy (Wood 1995). It had high visual impact; the plate was a palette and the dish a sculpture, a work of art. While nouvelle cuisine supposedly repudiated the excesses of traditional haute cuisine by dismissing heavy sauces that confused the flavors and over-large portions that appealed to the gastronomically greedy, it was still a form of excess. The chef became an artist, food became sculptural, and the cuisine was lauded as if it were a redemptive gesture. The chef was offering more than food; this was an invitation into the realms of the exquisite and aesthetic where the prosaic was transformed into the transcendent. This level of self-conscious artistry, delicacy and integrity of properly prepared dishes was a form of excess in itself.

The interest in food as entertainment parallels the economic boom of the 1850s to 1870s, particularly in the industrialized societies where the new professions of bankers, industrialists and service providers began driving the consumer economy. The growth of the middle classes is estimated to have doubled between 1830 and 1880; in the UK, for instance, it made up 20 percent of the entire population. New entertainments arose in response to the consumer power of this social class. The city of Bath, with its Grand Pump Room, offered refreshments in the style of tables d'hôte (food of the day) to a rapidly increasing number of tourists. Then the grand hotels developed along the English Riviera; the Torquay in 1863 and the Imperial Hotel in 1864, and in the city of London, Brown's in Vere Street and the Langham were established in 1865 (Burnett

2004: 67–75). Food was being elevated to the aesthetic, fashionable and exotic. In the mid-nineteenth century, the Café Royal on Regent Street opened near the theater district, department stores began offering refreshments, and glamorous tea shops such as Lyons at 213 Piccadilly became centers of entertainment. Burnett (2004: 123–4) has described the lavish interiors of these establishments where the food was predominantly baked goods and sourced externally from the new Aerated Bread Company (ABC). The early tea shops were not kitchens, but dispensers of foodstuffs; they arranged their offering in fashionably styled settings. Lyons, for instance, had Louis XVI decor, a gold fascia advertising board outside, and inside there were red silk walls, gas-lighted chandeliers, plush chairs and uniformed waiters. Other stylish places provided grand marble staircases and painted ceilings. The decor was superior to the comestibles, yet the presence of food, regardless of its simplicity and quality, provided the reason for the existence of these new public venues.

The restaurant experience supports the strengthening of our contemporary visual culture; it is a highly engineered site that employs myriad visual devices to enhance itself. Global franchised restaurants develop iconic appearances that function as a brand; the golden arches is the frequently cited example, but there are dozens – the Brown Derby, White Castle, KFC and Starbucks. In an era of intense visuality, the representation of food has taken on a vivid dimension. It is this growing emphasis on display with the items and practices of conspicuous consumption that forms a strong link between the human body and restaurants. In essence, the manner of eating performs identity, and eating in public re-positions the private into the public domain and heightens attention to our social conduct, manners, physical appearance and sense of fashion.

THE BODY AS SPECTACLE

We have inherited an intellectual tradition in which the fashioned body, free of all imperfections, has been regarded as a necessary component of human happiness (Thomas 2009: 228). Originally conceived by the ancient physiognomists as a combination of the primary elements earth, water, air and fire that made up all life forms, the visible body was an amalgam of properties that determined character and proclivities. How the body moved, the gait, height, weight, skin coloring, and shape of the skull were features that told of specific character traits. Less visible aspects such as moodiness, health, vigor and intelligence could also be read from physical signs: depression, for instance, could be seen in the heavy earthy shape of the limbs, and a propensity for happiness could be seen in the height of the forehead and the rising curvature of the eyebrows. These particular interpretations of physical features seem quaint now, even though we still regard physical appearance as telling. We read some features of the body in order to deduce personal qualities, even if we no longer accept the strict rules of the pre-modern physiognomists. Thin hair, baldness, too much hair in the wrong places, sunken eyes, small eyes, round face, short fingers, crooked teeth and so on are variously interpreted as signs of degeneration, failure of vitality, poor self-maintenance and lack of care. These body hot spots are targets for massive advertising campaigns selling hair tonics, color restoratives, skin creams for regeneration, diet and weight loss products, whitening toothpastes and detox elixirs.

Dozens of advertisements mix images of food, the body and identity to create tropes of successful living. Underlying these interconnections are the discredited theories of physiognomy and eugenics that have circulated through western culture for centuries. The body is taken as a sign of character on the assumption that the unique essence of an individual is reflected in the eyes, nose, face, hands, ears, jawline and forehead. Aristotle suggested, in a pre-psychology universe, that there were revealing connections between external physical features and hidden moral character. In particular, if the individual had a close physical resemblance to a bird, donkey, cow, snake and so on, then these features told of similar traits: an individual who resembled an owl or bull also shared their disposition. Those resembling a lion were thought to be strong but hot-tempered; a leopard was proud and deceitful as well as daring. Animals were described in terms of human qualities and they reappeared in humans bearing some animalistic features: "The wild boar is full of senseless rage, while the ox is simple and sincere. The horse likes pomp and craves honours. The fox is deceitful and scheming; the monkey likes joking and imitating. Sheep are self-assured; goats are lecherous; pigs are dirty and greedy." If individuals appeared similar to an animal in any feature, then they were assumed to have the associated mannerisms (Magli 1989: 101–3).

In the long history of physiognomic reasoning, the relationship between human identity and character and physical features reached popular proportions in the eighteenth-century work of Johann Caspar Lavater (1741–1801), who provided a systematic analysis of physical characteristics as a guide to sociability. He claimed that intellectual capacity and moral inclinations were all discernible in every part of the human body. It was thus important that we all became schooled in the tenets of physiognomy, Lavater urged, as it would improve the accuracy of the judgments we make of another person, especially at the first meeting. By following his systematic directions, we could become more scientific and reliable in our reading of the other's temperament and moral qualities. He answered the frequent concern that his method could not detect the deliberate attempts of a knowing individual to disguise or mislead others by explaining that certain body parts could not lie: the shape of the skull, eye color and the thickness of the lips were fixed and reliable signs of true character. In Lavater's schema, Mick Jagger and Angelina Jolie would both be obvious degenerates. In the present consumer age, the physical size and shape of the body are closely observed by various industries that market products capable of reshaping the body in accord with prevailing images of health and beauty. The technical means for such include cosmetic surgery to reshape the face, steroids for building musculature, botox injections and implanted prosthetics for correcting the profile, and in the near future, cloned spare body parts. Such techniques for remodeling the body and reinventing a self-image are becoming increasingly accessible to the affluent consumer, but the desire for such pre-dates the technology.

The value of self-fashioning has circulated through Western culture for centuries in various tales of transformation. The literature of the nineteenth century provides examples such as *The Picture of Dorian Gray*, *Dr Jekyll and Mr Hyde*, and *The Flying Dutchman*, to name a few. The desire for reinvention also has currency in reality television programs that have become popular in recent decades. Such entertainments tap into a generalized willingness to undertake demanding tasks in order to gain the prize of transformation; these requests are not unlike the Herculean challenges of *The Iliad* and *Odyssey* where the hero wins the golden prize by undertaking extreme feats of bravery. Changing appearance through self-fashioning and body modification in the form of reconstructive surgical procedures is an extreme process that produces unusual levels of pain. Dental realignment, face lifts, dermabrasions to remove tattoos, scars and wrinkles, liposuction, hair transplants, and breast augmentations and reductions are increasingly accepted. The extremity of such practices has been dramatized by performance artists such as Orlan and Stelarc who subject their own bodies to invasive procedures as a means of highlighting the plasticity of the body.

Whether it is changing fashions in clothing and lifestyle activities, or undergoing transformative procedures, the accepted ethos is that the body is a commodity to be shaped at will. What we do with the body, how we sustain and groom it, supports vast commercial interests, and as a result it is the focal point for a great deal of attention and hyperbole. Here is evidence of the ironic connection between the growth in the restaurant business and the contemporary emphasis on physical appearance. Both form part of the display of privacy in the public arena, and both have been industrialized and engineered in order to support a variety of spin-offs related to the manufacture of social identity.

SELF-FASHIONING

In May 2009, 250 years after Lavater, Susan Boyle stepped onto the stage of the popular television competition, *Britain's Got Talent*, where she was immediately and universally recognized as a failure. She was middle-aged, her face was flat and square, her hair unruly, her clothes unfashionable, her body shape thick. She was physically awkward and slightly dishevelled. There was a palpable ripple of disbelief and embarrassed laughter through the studio audience as she prepared to perform. They were used to seeing entertainers who were young, quirky to some extent, but still recognizable as attractive models. In a few brief seconds, after Susan began to sing, the mood altered; the television cameras swung towards the audience and registered a raft of mildly astonished faces. The judges of the talent program were screened and their expressions mirrored that of the audience. The previously dismissive first impressions were replaced with an apologetic chastisement. Twelve months after this initial television appearance, Susan Boyle was rich and famous. The video of her initial television appearance registered over a hundred million hits on YouTube, making it one of the most popular of all time. Her story has been revised, re-evaluated and re-positioned through various popular media reports. Her television appearances (Piers Morgan, *This is Your Life*, 31 December 2010) now reveal a more groomed, less visibly discreditable individual. The tell-tale signs that originally figured her as unconventional have been refined.

Shortly after the Susan Boyle episode of *Britain's Got Talent*, the prestigious TLS (*Times Literary Supplement*) featured a review of a scholarly book, *Writing Lives*, published by Oxford University Press (*TLS*, 17 July 2009). The review essay was headed "Be What You Seem" and the text occupied a full page, surrounding a color picture of Susan Boyle in full song, as she first appeared on the television talent show. The article made no mention of Susan Boyle; nonetheless, the image was apposite.

The book under review contained commentaries about identity and biography from the early modern period in England. The contributors addressed the organizing motif of biographical writing and self-representation, and variously outlined how this style of writing, dating from the Renaissance to the early modern period, had emphasized the importance of self-fashioning in a manner not unlike the contemporary postmodern discourses that focus on a decentered, fragmented and constructed human character. The style of writing in the Renaissance literature was closely related to the type of didactic manuals we now find in the self-help section of the high street bookstore. They gave instructions on how to be socially successful. They were less occupied with physiognomic revelations that exposed the nature of a deep-seated core identity and more interested in identity as a patinated construct, an assemblage of working guises as we would find now described in contemporary discourses written through a Foucauldian lens.

The different conceptions of identity addressed in Renaissance and Enlightenment writing demonstrate a polarized position taken towards the self that is now largely familiar to a contemporary audience. On the one hand, identity is accepted as a social tool fashioned through spin, and on the other hand, it is an essence that can be made visible through styles of acting and physical appearance. The positions are encapsulated in the juxtaposed phrases of the *TLS* essay in question, "be what you seem", which provides the headline for the essay, and the alternate position attributed to opponents of the fashioned image, "be rather than seem".

The case of Susan Boyle demonstrates the irreconcilable elements of these opposed perspectives; in her raw form, she struggled for acceptance and recognition and was not at all what she seemed to be, and then, in her refreshed persona, re-fashioned with a new haircut and set of clothes, she has become another person. She is now a celebrity capable of earning considerable sums of money as well as popular reputation. Initially she could not be herself because her appearance belied her character, but with the right spin, she has become what she now seems: a groomed, controlled and professional commodity.

The idea that we are as we appear is regularly challenged, but nonetheless persists as a widely held belief that organizes much of everyday social life. We may have inherited a view of the bourgeois subject as possessing a coherent, stable personality but, in the consumer era of self-fashioning, we are also skilled actors capable of presenting ourselves exactly as we wish to appear. The gist of the matter is enunciated by the character, Henry Wotton, in *The Picture of Dorian Gray* by Oscar Wilde (1966: 32): "it is only shallow people who do not judge by appearances. The true mystery of the world is the visible, not the invisible". We continuously act out and fashion an identity in order to produce a socially reliable and appropriate image. Thus what we appear to be is what we are for that moment. What you see is what you get, as is so commonly stated. At the same time, we know we are acting and so might everyone else be; hence, to accept the surface performance not as a performance is to make the mistake of accepting the sign for the thing itself, as Foucault (1983: 22) instructs: "signs invoke the very thing of which they speak". These ideas have relevance to our contemporary infatuation with the public sphere as an appropriate site in which to express private passions.

The consumer age is drenched with the view that the image is reality; that character is immanent in appearance, a viewpoint that has had a remarkably enduring legacy, from Aristotle to the Surrealists, to the twentieth-century public relations spin-doctors and beyond. The human body, like other commodities, is made intelligible through its appearance. How we look is a passport to social acceptability. Powerful industries promulgate these views in order to merchandize products from clothing and food products to pharmaceuticals and cosmetic surgery. Thus, perfecting the body is a means of shaping social opportunities and displaying identity even though the underlying logic of these connections draws on the much-disputed views of a physiognomic legacy.

THE IMAGE AND THE ICON

Food, the body, identity, self-representation and images of good health and vitality work together in tight lockstep to promote a wide array of consumer activities. Visual images of food and the body abound and draw on a highly valued cultural legacy in Western art. The works of Giuseppe Arcimboldo (1527–1593) combine food with the human form in painted portraits that appear both realistic and conventional when viewed at a distance, but on closer inspection, are composed of scientifically accurate plants, animals, fish and objects. Arcimboldo made the fantastic into the familiar; he transformed fruit into a portrait of summer, fish into a representation of water and birds into an image of air. His paintings appear conventional, but close up, the parts are separable and do not add up to the whole. These portraits are clever in their technical execution and humorous in their composition. They connect the human with the non-human, with animals, fish, birds and plants, in a continuity that pre-dates the Darwinian universe.

Arcimboldo was popular in his own time and his playful representations of nature and social forms continue to speak across the centuries as a statement of the unlimited influence of the image, and of the capacity of perspective to engender new meanings. His art has made the later work of the twentieth-century Surrealists and Dadaists seem all the more intelligible. He blurred definitions of the real and made them subject to perceptions – what is in the eye of the beholder. The juxtaposition of the incongruous made space, several hundred years later, for Meret Oppenheim's (1913–1985) sculpted fur-lined teacup. The power of this particular image captured a popular view circulating through the zeitgeist that connected the visceral sensation of revulsion with the banal. When the fur teacup was exhibited in 1936, the European world was on the verge of eugenic cleansing; ordinary people were soon to be re-imagined as vermin and become non-human. They were to be exterminated before they could contaminate the future utopian state. Revulsion was becoming a characterizing sentiment of the times, and may well have contributed to the instant success that greeted Oppenheim's art (see http://www.surrealists.co.uk/oppenheim.php).

The ordinary-sized cup, saucer and spoon were covered with the animal fur of a Chinese gazelle. The fur was wrapped around the cup's edge in such a way that it provided a thin lip, a shape widely accepted as indicating aesthetic good taste in a fine quality bone china teacup. A thin-lipped cup meant the drinker need open the mouth only slightly. A wide-open mouth suggests gulping and greed and hence incivility. Yet to drink from a fur teacup, even one with an elegant thin lip, was unappealing and even abhorrent. As an object, the fur teacup evokes some humor, but on second and third consideration it is increasingly repellent and menacing. It is an image that evokes a high level of anxiety about an ordinary activity like drinking. It suggests that what we are offered to ingest (to accept and swallow) literally and figuratively may not be healthy or good for us. Similarly, other works from the Surrealists such as René Magritte's *Masked Apples* carry many of the same ambiguous ideas about ordinary concepts. The strange image of apples wearing masks as if they were human faces draws attention to the problem of appearances. Are these apples identical? Are they a double or twin? Does the mask hide their identity or provide it? The point is that images are unlimited; they produce other images and in so doing generate more points of view.

Art and representation have the capacity to reveal properties of the social world without there necessarily being a correspondence between the image and fact. The ubiquity of the image joins illusion and reality so the world we know may exist wholly in the imaginary (Gombrich 1960). Every day we translate the prosaic into the mythological in order to have the world we want: driving a car becomes an act of freedom, drinking whisky a sign of masculinity, dining out an act of social success. Images can be so realistic and convincing that they become dominant, iconic and singular, and displace alternate versions (Kemp 2012). This is the dimension of hyperreality described by Umberto Eco: the fake is so appealing that it is better than the real.

When food is elevated to this level of spectacle, it too becomes a hyperreality, part of the mythological universe found in the everyday. When the invented, metaphoric image becomes part of everyday life, when the metaphor is literalized as reality, then the silent ideologies of the day become harder to see. The imposition of the image over the real is not the result of well-orchestrated strategies of propaganda and ideological manipulation but, instead, a consequence of excess, of the saturation of the everyday with images that constantly interpellate us and produce a cacophony of silent languages through which commodities, moral positions and social relations are continuously enunciated. Thus we arrive at the situation where it is difficult to see any object or social practice stripped of its multiple layers of symbolic meaning and pared down to its essential functions. This is not to suggest that objects and practices should be positioned outside culture (as if they could) but, rather, to bring attention to the density of images and representations that some objects accrue and, in particular, to bring attention to the successful transformation of food into a carrier of a multiplicity of social imperatives.

Humor around food is part of its cultural currency, from the cream pie thrown in the face of the silent actor in early Hollywood films to the much-quoted and now iconic scene in the diner in *When Harry Met Sally* (1989). Food is a language that has been readily harnessed to convey basic social values such as the re-installation of binary gender differences. Take the example of a recent advertisement for a male deodorant called Axe: the advert begins with a young man standing in front of a bathroom mirror, spraying Axe deodorant under his arms and across his chest. In a flash, he suddenly becomes a full-sized chocolate man with a wide toothy grin reminiscent of the clownish images of the golliwog used in early American advertising. Our Axe man, now transformed into a chocolate figure, finds himself walking through the streets of a busy city, drawing the attention of attractive young women who immediately want to devour him. Chocolate is, after all, a substance women crave and cannot refuse. As he passes two women eating on the street, he breaks off his nose and sprinkles it onto their ice cream cones; next he is seated in a darkened cinema, with a young woman on each side of him nibbling his ear and cheek; the advertisement continues with the chocolate man at the bedside of a young woman in hospital. He offers her an open chocolate box that contains a giant hand with moving fingers couched against satin lining. Several more rom-com scenarios are depicted in which the chocolate man is variously adored, hungered after and consumed. The associations of the body with food, of desire with chocolate, and sex with eating, are themes of this advertisement and many others (retrieved 1 January 2011 from http://www.dailymotion.com/video/x6u7ue_new-axe-dark-temptation-commercial_fun).

The sweet biscuit Tim Tam, made by Arnotts, used two advertisements that elide gender with food and exploit the differences in values held by men and women. The text reads in part: "A Tim Tam is better than a man because it's hard on the outside but has a soft centre ... when you finish with one, there's plenty more where that came from... . It'll satisfy you every time. What more could you want?" In the next version: "A Tim Tam is better than a woman because ... it won't complain if you have more than one at a time ... it exists only to bring you pleasure and expects nothing in return ... you can always find one when you want it. It'll always make you feel good. What more could you want?"

Food has lent itself to a variety of art forms, from the sixteenth-century paintings of Arcimboldo in which fruit, fish, animals and flowers created playful portraits of the human face, to its use in advertisements for a wide range of consumer products. From the elegantly photographed chicken, seafood, cherries and trifle that regularly appear in popular women's magazines to the gastro-porn of the cinema, food demonstrates its transformative capacity. It is no longer nourishment but ornamentation; it expresses illusions and hidden values such as the "dream of smartness" (Barthes 1972: 80).

The message that food conveys to the aspiring middle classes is that food is an art form, and art is culture, and culture is status, and status is a key to personal happiness. The power of food to generate cultural values begins to explain the mystery of how French haute cuisine came to dominate the middle-class culture in late modernity for almost a century and, furthermore, how any food style — irrespective of whether it is haute cuisine, the ingeniously packaged chocolate snack bar, or the American hamburger and French fries — can become a dominant global icon that conveys complex social messages across the spectrum from political ideology to the cultivation of personal tastes and habits.

MARKETING FOOD

The association of food and social class has a long history that is still evident in contemporary society. In the seventeenth century, tea gardens at Vauxhall and Ranelagh connected the fashion-conscious classes on parade with the imbibing of spring waters and simple refreshments. In the bustling coffee houses of London, Paris and New York, mixing food with commerce and sociability became the fashion. In London, the coffee house flourished from the 1660s; in Paris, it multiplied in the next century: in 1789 there were about 100 restaurants and in 1804 about 500, and by 1835 more than a thousand (Burnett 2004: 2). Their immense popularity combined conviviality and the consumption of food and drink with critical commentaries on the indulgence of these social habits. Burnett notes a fashion in the nineteenth century for writing about food in a satirical and humorous manner: Tabitha Tickletooth was the pseudonym for Charles Selby writing about the food question in the popular press. Another widely read fashionable text of 1855 was *Memoirs of a Stomach, Written by Himself, That all who eat may read*, edited by a Minister of the Interior.

Food has a history of being central to cultural production as it is taken for granted as a necessity for social survival.

The practices we follow around food demonstrate social position, cultural capital and ideological views. Where we eat, with whom, when and in what style are details that address the contemporary issues of food manufacture and distribution as well as the vested interests that support global food industries. In such a context, connections are readily drawn between consumer practices and the body and, in this instance, between the Michelin-starred restaurant and representations of the oversized human body. These associations report on the lavish attention given to detailing food preparation as a form of entertainment (as demonstrated in popular programs beginning four decades ago with *The Galloping Gourmet* up to the contemporary *Master Chef*, *My Kitchen Rules* and *Come Dine With Me*), and the equally comprehensive attention given to diet and health regimes. As consumers of both representations, we are the point of focus as the free, autonomous beings that pursue personal happiness and fulfilment through a variety of consumer habits.

The advent of the diet industries identified the overweight body as a site of moral opprobrium that is often used to suggest psychological malady. The advanced industrial economies now identify widespread obesity as an epidemic and serious threat to the economic fabric. Statistics about its prevalence are quoted to show that over-eating is more common than under-nutrition. The International Association for the Study of Obesity (IASO), founded in the 1960s, has been accumulating data for the past five decades, and states that worldwide there are 475 million obese adults, with another 900 million or more who are overweight, giving a total of 1.5 billion adults with health risks arising from being overweight. In adults, the trends indicate that during the 1990s the number of obese men almost trebled from 6 percent of the population in 1980 to 17 percent in 1998, and for women much the same; 8 percent in 1980 and 21 percent in 1998 (Burnett 2004: 326). Such evidence is used to predict that the 200 million school-age children who are overweight will probably have shorter lifespans than the previous generation (www.iaso.org). According to Eric Schlosser (2002: 242), children consume 17.6 kilograms of chocolate per year, 6.4 kilograms of savory snacks per year, 6.3 kilograms of chilled desserts such as ice cream and frozen yogurt and 4.5 kilograms of sweet biscuits. The spread of obesity in children is largely confined to the Americas and Western Europe, with much lower, almost negligible evidence in Africa and parts of Asia. However, as fast foods with high fat and sugar content (such as hamburgers, fries and chocolate) become more fashionable and popular with the young in the Westernizing cities of Asia, the trend toward obesity in children is becoming evident. Estimates are that one in five children are affected by excess body weight and this rate is higher in Greece, the USA and Italy (http://dx.doi.org/10.1787/health_glance-2011-19-en).

The obese body has been observed in the ancient and early modern worlds (Venus of Willendorf, Chaucer's Friar Hubbard, St Thomas Aquinas, Shakespeare's Falstaff), and the physical health of the body has been an acknowledged site of instruction; for example, at the Roman baths (*Mens sana in corpore sano* – a sound mind in a clean and healthy body; *Mede agan* – nothing in excess). These ancient directives were clear: health derived from a balanced, moderate diet and active lifestyle. The shape of the body was integral to the mind; the assumption was that a healthy regimen produced a moral life. This particular view of human fulfilment has been slowly eroded with the spread of affluence in the contemporary West.

Re-making the world through scientization, mercantile capitalism, industrialization and liberal democracy has also re-made the human body. The modern individual is encouraged to pursue self-fulfilment through the consumer pleasures found in a materialistic society. These in turn reward the individual with a sense of autonomy and authenticity associated with the cult of self-expression. J.S. Mill famously pronounced that individualism was good for the species, that variety in character, experimentation in living and the free development of capacities were the ingredients of a fulfilled existence. Such sentiments have been echoed by most of the intellectual giants of Western culture: Marx, Kierkegaard, Nietzsche, Hegel, Sartre and Freud (Thomas 2009: 11–12). Yet the intellectual traditions that advocate ideal ways of living are divided between secular and religious views of the body, each pronouncing on alternate ways to live a respectable life. The latter suggest that the body is an imperfect vessel that will be restored to a state of perfection after a proper death, while the secular view describes the body as a vessel that enables human fulfilment on earth through the cultivation of the mind (Thomas 2009: 228).

From both perspectives, the body is the center of attention and thus has come to be exposed to the scrutiny of expert professionals who continuously investigate its physical, mental and moral fitness. The body has become an acknowledged sign of the self and an extension of character. In our contemporary consumer society, this makes the unconventional body, especially the obese body, a figure of censure and ridicule, as if its stigmatised proportions represent a lack of psychological balance and self-discipline.

Less visible in this picture is recognition of the ambivalent perspectives toward the body that underlie the vast commercial interests involved with the global economy of food development, production and distribution. Some estimates record the fast food industry in America turning over more than $120 billion annually (Foer 2009). This alone makes food big business but, in addition, food is a source of innovation in the biotechnology industries that are focused on engineering new food substances, as well as in techniques for expanding agribusiness that maximize profitability. Sustaining the human body provides the impetus for a great deal of business development, whether it is feeding the starving body with engineered crops or attempting to starve the obese body through pharmaceutical products that tamper with the brain chemistry and change signals of hunger into signs of surfeit.

During the 1990s, a significant increase in genetically modified foods came onto the market. Some of these were identified on food labels and others were not. The consumer uptake varied in countries largely as a result of consumer trust in government regulatory agencies and a more general trust and acceptance of the benefits of science itself. In the USA, the household consumer was familiar with processed and packaged foods and accepted the value of the regulatory Food and Drug Administration (FDA). In contrast, in the UK and Europe, recent events have undermined the consumer trust in government bodies. After the Chernobyl accident and the food safety scares associated with various forms of contamination and degradation, there was a more widespread perception that governmental agencies were neither capable nor willing to ensure quality control. In turn, this added further suspicion to foods that were produced through novel technology such as genetic engineering. By the end of the 1990s, there were deeply divided opinions about the benefits of bioengineered foods. While positive consequences might include better production and reduced cost, with the associated possibility of reducing the incidence of severe hunger in certain countries, on the negative side there were lingering suspicions that these changes in food production would inevitably increase the wealth and influence of large corporations and big business by treating humans as guinea pigs (Baghurst 2007). The public response to new farming techniques such as feeding herbivore cows meat-based products has led to mass media reports about the mysterious and surprising origins of some food products. Media headlines about "cannibal cows" and "Frankenfoods" exist alongside the ubiquitous restaurant review and newspaper column advising on health and diet.

Pharmaceutical companies are heavily engaged in both the body image and the food business insofar as there is a large market for medications that assist with appetite control and weight loss. For instance, new drugs for use in weight control are frequently introduced to the market with the approval of the FDA in America. These are mostly successful and produce substantial returns for the pharmaceutical companies. At the same time, many of these drugs also produce dangerous side effects and become the cause of class action legal suits (Nestle 2002). New food products such as snack foods can also have unanticipated consequences that produce large-scale social problems. Snack foods have increased solo eating and reduced sociability around food. They also account for the prevalence of childhood obesity as an increasing public health problem. Within such a context, marketing campaigns often highlight the health benefits of foods, and now all manner of commodities make claims for enhancement to health and vitality. Additives to milk and fruit juices are commonplace; vitamin supplements for children have been introduced on the assumption that regular meals do not provide these necessary ingredients. There are even vitamin-added food products for the domestic pet. Marketing campaigns use the trope of good health to sell products that promise to deliver such benefits.

The function of advertising is to influence consumer practices. Food advertising, in particular, is a large segment in the expenditure of the food industry. Nestle (2002: 22) noted that food marketers downplay the significance of advertising by arguing there is so much advertising in the marketplace that the consumer is not influenced by any single advertisement or representation. Yet Nestle has also observed that food sales increase with the intensity, repetition and visibility of an advertised message. A great deal of food advertising is directed at children who have a less active critical capacity to evaluate the nutritional value of a food product; they are presumably more influenced by the representation of the product and the social narrative that surrounds it than its health value. Soft drinks, ice creams, individually packaged biscuits and snacks have been designed and marketed to young consumers and the consequence has been an increase in their vulnerability to food-related health disorders.

FOOD, ART AND THE BODY

All signs and symbols are both full and empty, thus forcing us, the spectator, to struggle to find meaning. Roland Barthes (1972: 78–80) exemplifies this with his commentary on the images of ornamental cooking that regularly appear in popular women's magazines. He took the example of the glossy images of advertised food that were intended to sell the benefits of domesticity to the bourgeois housewife. The lacquered chicken that glistens

141

in the glossy photograph alongside the recipe makes food into a highly aestheticized object. By drawing attention to this style of advertising, Barthes was making the point that these images were promoting a class system based on political and economic interests. In this instance, food was an effective vehicle for circulating the message that home cooking is a sign of domestic harmony; that the happiness of the married suburban couple is to be found in the well-prepared chicken dish. Simon Schama (2004: 10) has stated that all art forms replace reality and do not reproduce it. Art is a currency for reading the world; it is a cultural summation of all that we know. As a result, when we privilege some art forms over others, we also establish a hierarchical ranking of different knowledge systems.

In *Cloning Terror* (2004), the picture theorist W.J.T. Mitchell proposes that some images burst out of their frame and become substitutes for reality. He cites the images of "the man on the box" from the Abu Ghraib prison, the destruction of the huge Buddhist idols and the twin towers of the World Trade Center in Lower Manhattan as instances where the image has produced further images and metaphors that in turn have become as important as the original acts (Costello and Willsdon 2008: 6). The domination of the image has led some artists to warn us that visual representations are not the same as the real object: Andy Warhol's painted Campbell's soup cans and René Magritte's painting of a pipe remind us that the image is not the reality – *Ceci n'est pas une pipe*. Without these reminders, the image can be hard to distinguish from the reality. Yet by noting how food has been translated into images that enjoy global recognition, we are reminded of the influence of the hyperreal and of how receptive we have become to visual suggestions carried through fashionable objects.

Art has the capacity to show how the prevailing interpretations of the world are constructed. It can make the object into a subject and invite us to look again at the canvas or sculpture and consider the messages being delivered. Next, art unbalances those messages and makes the object of the work into a subject, into a site where other meanings can emerge and be considered. Every art object, every imagistic depiction begins as an interpretation that initiates an interrogation of the obvious and in so doing begins a spiral process in which meanings are examined, re-examined and re-ordered. So when food becomes a fashionable image of itself, a hyperreality, then its image subverts its own appearance and in so doing can reveal the existence of other meanings behind the surface. The image of food, like all art forms, shapes public opinions, and where the image is highly effective as with Arcimboldo's portraits, Magritte's apples, Oppenheim's teacup, Warhol's soup cans and Edward Burra's snack bar, then food itself has become detached and free-floating, able to be associated equally well with the sublime and the disgusting.

This effect of the image connects the extremes of the Michelin-starred restaurant and the modern obese body insofar as both attract the hyperbole of a cultural system that has transformed food into widely recognized popular icons in order to sell it as entertainment, not necessarily sustenance. After all, the natural body – in its various activities of eating, sleeping, walking and talking – is always a cultural product, and as such it reveals much of the social context in which we live. Thinking about food and the body draws together the hyperbole that surrounds them both in the consumer-oriented West. There is an elective affinity between them, and as a consequence they are both highly visible spectacles in which our appetites for the perfect meal and the perfect body have become fused. Instances of obesity have been recorded for centuries but it is only recently that it has been conceived as a social threat. It is now condemned as evidence of abundance, over-production, gluttony, excess and lack of discipline. At this point, there is a convergence of interest in food, its image, the consumer, health and marketing. The dominance of visuality in contemporary culture and the ubiquity of advertising images that consistently link food with physical pleasures bring emphasis to the body as a site of self-invention and moral valuation. Consumption of food in a Michelin-starred restaurant, or snacking too much in front of television, is a trope of contemporary society inextricably tied with self-image and self-presentation.

5 THE ANOMIC CONSUMER

All the conditions of modern life – its material plenitude, its sheer crowdedness – conjoin to dull our sensory faculties.

SUSAN SONTAG

The painting by Patrick Caulfield, *After Lunch* (1975), depicts a resting figure, looking into an empty dining room. He appears tired, drooping pensively over a serving hatch; he is turned away from the picture postcard scenery of mountains, lakes and fairytale castle towers framed by the restaurant's window. Instead he gazes over the scene inside the restaurant, an empty room. It is the hour after lunch; the restaurant is closed in between opening again for the next service. The painting gives color to the external world of the natural landscape, the bright sunshine makes the water sparkle and the air is clear enough to see distant mountains. In contrast, the interior dining room of the restaurant is painted in a bland blue tint. The chairs, tables, light fittings, walls, floor and ceiling are emptied of detail and flattened into a two-dimensional surface. Caulfield marks the differences between the natural and social landscapes, giving texture and vividness to one and not the other. The painting effectively takes us behind the scene to raise the question of what follows after lunch, after the event, after the rituals of the entertainment have been played out. The painting asks – what remains? – and in this instance, it is a tired worker and a bland space without human animation. The painting juxtaposes the brilliance of the external natural world, seen through the picture window and painted in vivid color against the flat blue interior of the restaurant, and in so doing we are given the suggestion that the colorful vibrancy of the world lies outside the restaurant.

Caulfield's painting challenges Jean Anthelme-Brillat-Savarin's nineteenth-century gastronomic aphorisms reporting on the pleasures of dining by highlighting the aftermath of the meal. While the restaurant supposedly provides a variety of diversions and indulgences, Caulfield's view offers a look behind the scenes and a perspective that suggests that the real sparkle of life lies outside in the vibrant real world and not in the lifeless etching depicting the inside of the restaurant.

SELF-ABSORPTION

A consumer culture promotes the pursuit of pleasure. Zygmunt Bauman has argued that the driving force in human society is not for us to attain our dreams but to keep dreaming, forever thinking about and hoping for a future in which greater pleasures will be available. It is not possession that we value but the desire to possess. To live in a state of desire makes us feel engaged; it defies entropy. The advent of the consumer society has amplified these emotions by constantly asserting the value of distraction and of our always being in a state of longing. Conspicuous consumption supports insatiability and the undesirability of reaching completion and surfeit. Consumerism is driven by the continual invention of new desires and the renewed wish to feel liberated from banal occupations. Daily life is thus an engagement with activities that repudiate a sense of finality and offer instead a future of endless excitement. The consumer ethic promises to deliver such thrills without losing freshness and purpose. It promises that there will always be more; the search will continue as "it is the hunting, not the hare that people call happiness" (Bauman 2001: 24).

Embedded in this ethic of insatiability is the transformation of every kind of experience into a commodity that can be purchased and made part of our social repertoire. Even politically correct positions – say, for greater concern with the environment – can become an opportunity for self-enhancement. Bauman gives the example of the middle-class response to reducing environmental pollution by not driving a car, which also serves the opportunity for fashioning an identity as a bicycle or scooter-rider who has a "Dolce and Gabbana leather jacket, Adidas red high-top trainers, a Gucci silver helmet or Jil Sander wrap-around sunglasses" (Bauman 2004: 84). It is a description not far removed from Dick Hebdige's caustic characterization of the unanchored subject. However, this is not the end state: Bauman also recognizes the value of the self-aware individual as a source of critical opposition to emotional capitalism and instrumental rationality. Such individuals develop by dismantling those deeply embedded humanist ideals that assume an autonomous subject. He implies a self-aware citizen is possible when it is understood that the road to that state lies through the morass of liquid modernity, that stultifying atmosphere where fleeting engagements, speed-dating and calculated relations dominate our social relations.

Foucault previously argued for much the same when he underscored the necessity to escape the mythologies perpetrated about identity by the carceral and disciplinary socio-political regimes of the West. Foucault argued that cultural conventions and fashionable practices mask their own effects; that is, they conceal the very phenomenon they address. For instance, identity is a concept we apply to ourselves as a mode of self-reference, but that process of referral does not necessarily supply definition or content. Thus, the self becomes an epistemic object; it corresponds to a role and set of assumptions that are continually referred to but lack both definition and stability. In a sense, then, it is fictional. If we could strip away the assumptions about identity and assert that it is not grounded in human nature nor is it contingent on historical and specific regimes of social practices, then the idea itself would become visible again only through a description of those modes of conduct, types of feelings, aspirations, sensations and pleasures and so on that are grouped together in a fictional unity as a causal principle known as a self. In short, behind the concept of identity there is an absence of knowledge. Were we to accept this position then the problematic concepts of identity and selfhood would evaporate but, at the same time, so might the consumer imperative to buy goods that advertise personality.

INVENTING THE SELF

The novel is credited with inventing the idea of the discoverable self, with highlighting the mechanics of consciousness and the manner with which we think through and solve the puzzles presented by the external chaotic world. Thinking is, after all, an acquired technique for the imposition of order. Popular entertainments from early novels to contemporary reality television programs function as primers in the art of establishing order. In the classical world, the novel seems to have been a plot-driven narrative. In the first novel, arguably *The Metamorphoses* (or *The Golden Ass*), written in Latin by Apuleius in the second-century AD, the hero encounters numerous adventures and challenges, not least of which is being transformed into a donkey and dealing with life's challenges from an animal's position. The ancient world provides examples where ideas of the self and the meaning of identity are acknowledged and debated as a strategy for addressing external challenges. It was not until Descartes's *cogito ergo sum* that a sustained argument about the nature and substance of this concept was disseminated across a more widely literate society (Martin and Barresi 2006). Skimming the intellectual distance between the ancient and Renaissance worlds reintroduces the novel form and dates its popular origins to a late sixteenth-century world in which the weakening of Christianity and its prohibitions against the inward journey toward self-consciousness allows an interest in writing and thinking about human nature to commence again (Greenblatt 1980).

From the late seventeenth and early eighteenth centuries in north-western Europe, cities grew in size, reaching populations of half a million and then beyond. These congregations of people provided opportunities for the pursuit of diverse pleasures and encouraged the formation of distinctive subcultures trafficking in a range of vices from the mild to the sensational. Segments of eighteenth-century fashionable and rich London society have been described as indulging in episodes of moral chaos as they followed their inner drives and passions and exploited the vulnerabilities of others. The mid-century was infamous for its cycle of perpetual masquerades and festivals where clandestine sexual adventures were encouraged by the fashion of literally disguising identity and going about in public shielded by anonymity. It appeared that the ostensible purpose of these public entertainments was to turn the sexual world upside down and engage in an assortment of indulgences without appending a diagnostic label to them. Thus, the erotic mix of men and women, masters and servants, homosexuals and transvestites produced an over-heated interest in the theatricality of identity without the consequent branding of these indulgences as a pathology of sexual proclivity or moral character. The display of unleashed eroticism permeated discussions in various social circles, and questions about human nature and the moral order became part of fashionable discourse. The problem of categorization, of how sexual desire could be contained by labels and discourses, fuelled a lurid imagination about the capacities of human desire once unleashed to indulge monstrous sexual aberrations such as hermaphroditism, nymphomania and priapism. There were extensive publications of pornography available and these too have contributed to a view of the *mentalité* of the early modern period in which individual identity was based in an erotic charge (Castle 1986; Hunt 1993).

The novel *Memoirs of a Woman of Pleasure*, better known as *Fanny Hill* (1748) by John Cleland, provides an account of organized prostitution as practiced at first in the relative privacy of Mrs Cole's well-known bagnio and then in the open, on the streets and in taverns and coffee houses of thriving London (Trumbach 1987: 76). Such literary depictions were not far removed from the realistic portraits of London street life painted by William Hogarth (1697–1764), for example, in *The Harlot's Progress*. Pickpockets, prostitutes and drunks populated the streets and a wide variety of tastes and appetites could be pursued without much apparent formal restraint. Against this narrative background of social competition was a general concern for estimating sincerity in others, and in knowing the truth of another's character. The mixing together of the social ranks brought with it a need to understand the nature of sociability and how an individual's character could be distilled from expressions and appearances. The experimental epistolary novel, *Pamela or Virtue Rewarded* by Samuel Richardson (1689–1761), appeared in 1740 and became an almost instant best-seller. It recounts through letters between a father and daughter the life of a servant girl climbing the social ladder and learning to resist and manage the many challenges to her virtue encountered along the way. The novel became a primer for young women who were aspiring to better social positions and who readily accepted Pamela's adventures as being based in fact. It was quickly followed by an anonymous satire published in 1741 with the title *An Apology for the Life of Mrs Shamela Andrews*, also known by its popular name, *Shamela*. Written by Henry Fielding (1707–1754) although published anonymously, it recounts the true events of the heroine who was not a chaste and kindly servant girl as Richardson described her but was, instead, a scheming actor who was deliberately attempting to entrap her wealthy master into marriage.

This concern for being as one appears (rather than seeming to be, see the previous discussion of Susan Boyle in Chapter 4) persists for a long time. In the next century, Jane Austen references it in *Mansfield Park* (1814) where the theatrical amusements created by Sir Thomas Bertram's young charges, while he is temporarily away from home, earn his immediate wrath on his return as they signal to him a dangerous interest in experimentation and the beginning of habits of dissemblance. From this willingness to play-act, there was assumed to be a logical slide into the disreputable use of disguise and self-fashioning for the expressed purpose of indulging private pleasures. These literary examples are important for measuring the temperature of the times as their popularity reveals a resonance with interests and sensibilities across the different segments of the reading public. It is an idea that gives credence to using the popularity of contemporary reality television programs as indicative of prevailing cultural values.

Both Terry Castle and Michel Foucault independently document the eighteenth century as an age where the display of identity was not limited by the assumptions of a given human nature but, on the contrary, was unleashed by the possibilities of experimentation. The privileged classes could play at being other than they were; it was a period when sexual impersonation was rife. In the eighteenth century, there were moments of radicalized sensibilities that grew from numerous opportunities for social experiments. For instance, there were popular accounts of transvestite escapades in which notorious individuals perpetrated effective disguises in order to live out their sexual, social and political adventures (Castle 1987: 157). An example was the colorful and enigmatic life of Chevalier d'Eon (1728–1810) who was variously a man, woman, spy, diplomat and soldier and as such provides a vivid example of the audacity of the era. This attractive and fashionable figure was well known in a wide social circle and resided for considerable lengths of time in the upper echelons of both London and Paris, where s/he demonstrated an ambiguous and sometimes incongruous sense of identity. At times, the Chevalier was a man who fought duels and went to war; at other times, indeed, for more than three decades, she was decidedly a woman who generated a good deal of gossip and notoriety. Aside from such accounts of extraordinary individuals – of which there are a number, including the strange case of Lord Cornbury, the Governor of New York and representative of the British Queen Anne (Garber 1992: 53) – the salient point is that the social and cultural tensions of the eighteenth century exemplified the important idea that society was only a convention, a fabrication that differed from nature and was importantly a product of fashion, a realm that could be shaped and styled at will.

To accept the idea that the conventions we take for granted are artificial and imaginary; that, in a sense, we live in a world of arbitrary forms that have emerged from recorded histories of endless possibilities, is to accept a level of distance and detachment that encourages scrutiny of everyday habits. When we accept the principle that the world is a cultural frame, we are better equipped to see its manner of manufacture. The legacy of Western culture in this regard can be described as a rigorous assault on our discoverable nature; that is, it is a history of investigation into human nature, biology, psychology and sociability.

Studies of gender have been particularly sensitive in measuring the cultural value placed on defining the natural body. A wide variety of accounts exist about the proper forms for masculinity and femininity and, in the popular literature that circulated through the eighteenth century, there are detailed descriptions that contravened contemporary views and would even challenge present-day attitudes. For example, the novel *The Man of Feeling*, published in 1771, described the ideal and proper masculine character; it was received by the public as a kind of sentimental blockbuster and sold out shortly after its publication (Todd 1986: 110). It described the manly hero as uninterested in commerce or making money and easily moved to emotional expressions such as weeping and softness in manners. The display of gentleness and sensibility was not a sign of effeminacy but the opposite, a view that might resonate now with the image of the new age, metrosexual male promoted through women's fashion and lifestyle magazines of the late twentieth century.

The cultural representations found in popular novels and entertainments give a sense of the general atmosphere of the eighteenth century where a degree of urgency colored the extremes of permissiveness and panic. As it became more acceptable to mingle across the social ranks of the privileged high and the canny low, it became more obvious that there was no logic to social position; instead, there was a growing recognition that arbitrary circumstances played a part. The narrative of Pride and Prejudice (1813) by Jane Austen illustrates this emerging view that the divide between social segments was not always desirable and that breaching these barriers could produce profound personal happiness – a position Michel Foucault would probably support equally forcefully. The displacement of a received social order strengthened the belief that we are "perverse by definition, sexually ambidextrous, and potentially unlimited in the range of (our) desires" (Castle 1987: 158). Our emotions, needs, sensibility and appetites are arbitrarily acquired and thus we are free to explore their variation and limits. With such an understanding, there can be an absence of constraint and that, in turn, provides the opportunity to escape "into new realms of voluptuous disorder" (Castle 1987: 161).

This bawdy background to the evolution of contemporary society poses questions about how the twenty-first-century metropolis has evolved into its relatively sedate and orderly state. The prescriptive literature on manners that began circulating from the fifteenth century, and continues to be conveyed through various popular media, provided instruction in the need to control bodily movements and to observe the other's style of conduct in order to reduce the possibility of giving offence. New social places like parks and restaurants were changing the character of the public domain in the eighteenth century into a space for parading oneself and meeting others – not always on the bustling metropolitan streets filled with thieves and pickpockets, but in the safer environments of cafés, restaurants and outdoor arcades. This revitalized interest in looking at one another in order to estimate personal qualities and sensibilities reinforced a view that character was a social and cultural phenomenon; it could be cultivated and styled from fashions that operated in a cunning manner to overcome and replace the dictates of nature.

The popular use of systems of observation such as Lavater's physiognomy tried to counter the anxiety generated by fashions for disguise and dissemblance. His system of character analysis demonstrated that certain obdurate qualities could not be hidden; thus, the criminal could not be concealed behind an elegant mode of dress, nor the worthy and honest provincial be wronged by unfashionable manners.

Lavater also urged that physiognomic reasoning itself be accepted as a natural property and that, in turn, meant all individuals were innately capable of understanding how bodily features connected to personal characteristics. To accept that self-fashioning and the production of character were features of human ingenuity meant that it was merely a matter of learning how to read these signs properly, and once we were in possession of these developed skills, the sense of anxiety produced by a belief that all appearances were misleading disguises could be comprehensively quelled (Wahrman 2004: 294–306).

THE BEGINNING OF COOL

The contradictory tensions between believing, on the one hand, that human nature was revealed in physiognomy and, on the other hand, that society and culture could overcome the dictates of nature and free the individual to become their fashioned self, were the ingredients of a generalized urgency to become more astute and better able to understand, at a glance, the character of the stranger. It was the beginning of the process of cooling down the eruptive and experimental social forms associated with the early modern period and preparing for the long evolution into the cold engineered environments of late modernity. The documented transformation of European hot cultures into cooler ones does not obviously begin with the Enlightenment, as there are earlier displays that reveal a widespread hot rustic rudeness. In two engravings after the style of Pieter Brueghel – The Ass In The School (1556) (http://www.1st-art-gallery.com/Pieter-The-Elder-Bruegel/ The-Ass-In-The-School-1556.html) and The Pedlar Pillaged by the Apes (1562) (http://rubens.anu.edu.au/htdocs/bytype/ prints/brueghel/0001/198.JPG) – there are scenes of undisciplined comportment and obscene acts depicted with the probable intention to both amuse the viewer and to moralize. Both portray the opposition between nature and culture; the mischievous band of monkeys are shown robbing the pedlar of his symbols of urban progress – dice, coins, keys, musical instruments, spectacles, silverware, gloves, a mirror, socks. The monkeys are human-like; there are two riding toy horses (center left), acting as if they were human children at play. The message is clearly about the thin divide between culture and nature, human and non-human.

The picaresque novel of Miguel de Cervantes, Don Quixote, marks a point of change in the representation of identity. Written between 1605 and 1615, Don Quixote is the story of an unhinged aristocrat and his everyman companion as they journey through the Spanish countryside. It is, at the same time, a journey into the interior, into the working mind of the imaginative, good-humored adventurer encountering the unpredictable world. As Christian doctrine waxes and wanes, such explorations are repeated again and again in the Western canon with William Congreve's *Incognita* (1692), Daniel Defoe's *Robinson Crusoe* (1719) and *Moll Flanders* (1722), Samuel Richardson's *Pamela* (1740) and its spoof *Shamela* (1741), Laurence Sterne's *Tristram Shandy* (1759–66), Goethe's *The Sorrows of Young Werther* (1774), Fanny Burney's *Evelina* (1778) and on to the twentieth century, Franz Kafka's *The Metamorphosis* (1915) and beyond. The search for meaning and order spawns different modes of mental organization and begins, from the nineteenth century, to produce a league of middle-class professionals who commercialize the search for personal meaning. Samuel Smiles (1812–1904), the author of numerous best-sellers including *Self Help*, *Character* and *Thrift*, is an early example of what we know in the middle-class West as the professional life-coach.

The contemporary consumer society has numerous industries dedicated to the cultivation, realization and expression of the self that link back to this long history underlying the transformation of identity into an asset that is subsequently re-formulated and presented back to us as a necessary part of our grooming for a successful social life (Greenblatt 1980; Thomas 2009). This groomed self is now very familiar, yet Western literature has not produced much consensus on its nature. As a result, our literary canon is replete with diverse narratives giving an account of how we might conduct our affairs: Niccolo Machiavelli (1469–1527) asserted that all human activities involve dissemblance and the better we are at creating a persona, the more influence we will enjoy over others; Baldessare Castiglione (1478–1529) argued that being

157

watchful and strategic must be our primary concern but, at the same time, these attributes must be concealed. The ease with which we manage the unexpected is a sign of our civility; such a capacity usually arises from a high level of self-consciousness. We must be capable of deft social parrying but we cannot appear to be designing or planning our actions. We must always appear to be spontaneous, uncomplicated and sincere; this is the art of self-invention. Castiglione referred to this talent as *sprezzatura*, an early form of what we would now refer to as "cool". We must appear accommodating, understanding and reasonable in order to seem genuine, and this level of poise will give us credible influence with others: this is the much-admired "art of being artless". Michel de Montaigne (1533–92) described human consciousness as "a room behind the shop", where the necessary fashioning of a public life was devised in the backstage, away from public view. More contemporary instances of self-fashioning and self-expression are found in the stream of consciousness fictions of James Joyce and Virginia Woolf. Examples are also found in Jean-Paul Sartre's philosophy of existentialism where the authentic individual is created by his or her own choice of actions, in Friedrich Nietzsche's instruction to "become the person you are", in Oscar Wilde's description of self-realization as the prime purpose in life, in Nicholson Baker's (1988) ruminations while riding an escalator in a shopping mall, and in Guy Debord's (1977: 4–18) descriptions of the individual as a theatrical prop in the society of the spectacle. Identity is a cultural form of self-absorption; it is part of the world of rumination, deception and impression management that lies behind the socially obvious and performed, and in this guise it has been repeatedly addressed by the West's canonical writers and artists (Thomas 2009).

Our cultural heritage illuminates the importance that appearances have assumed, especially at those times when the habits of self-fashioning became more widely adopted. The plasticity of appearances carries the disturbing message that fashioned dress is a disguise, whether it is intended to be or not, and that the conventions around appropriate conduct do not necessarily guarantee a reliable reading of the individual. Magritte represented this problem with the surrealist painting of the *Masked Apples* that begs the question: what is revealed or concealed by their appearance? Stephen Greenblatt (2004: 76) has described Elizabethan society as consumed with anxiety over the demonstrations of social position as a consequence of the wider circulation of ideas about self-fashioning:

> Elizabethan society was intensely, pervasively, visibly hierarchical: men above women, adults above children, the old above the young, the rich above the poor, the wellborn above the vulgar. ... The social elite lived in a world of carefully calibrated gestures of respect. They demanded constant, endlessly reiterated signs of deference from those below them: bowing, kneeling, doffing hats, cringing...

At the same time that these restrictions were in place, Greenblatt noted how individuals such as William Shakespeare's father could attempt to change their social position by reinventing themselves, by buying a past through the College of Heralds and passing themselves off as members of the idle gentry (Greenblatt 2004: 77). The plasticity of appearances has traveled into the present. The person on the high street, in military garb, wearing the camouflage outfit of the combat soldier, is probably not a soldier; to assume the figure wearing a frock is probably female is now less reliable after Judith Butler's (1990) comments on the pleasures of cross-dressing and drag. Consider again the case of Edward Hyde, immortalized in a portrait wearing a low-necked blue velvet dress and pale-colored gloves. He has a heavy beard and jowls, giving his face a distinctively masculine appearance. Despite some controversy over the authenticity of the portrait, it is supposedly Edward Hyde, Lord Cornbury, and Governor of New York and Jersey in America at the beginning of the eighteenth century. As cousin to the British Queen Anne and as her colonial representative, he is described as dressing in her image. While the portrait may suggest transvestism, he defended his appearance as an homage to the Queen – "You are very stupid not to see the propriety of it. In this place and particularly on this occasion I represent a woman [Queen Anne] and ought in all respects to represent her as faithfully as I can" (Garber 1992: 53). (See also http://www.historic-uk.com/CultureUK/edward-hyde-governor-NY.jpg.)

Many lives are passed following unchosen obligations within tradition-bound circumstances and such lives are dominated by habit and routine, subordinated by drudgery and difficulty. Such were the lives of nineteenth-century children, for example, who provided the cheap and plentiful labor force for the expanding industrial revolution in Britain. They had limited opportunities to question whether an autonomous identity existed and whether it was important. In contrast, most of us in the contemporary West seem to enjoy the luxury of exploring who we are and then making ourselves into what we want. A great deal of Western culture is infused with this quest to know and re-make ourselves. Yet, the question arises whether this kind of self-examination and self-discovery is a necessary technique for sustaining particular socio-economic regimes such as the consumer imperative, or whether it is a natural property of all humanity.

The journey inward into human consciousness took a decisive turn with the spread of trade, the rise of secularism and the growth of the commercial city. The individual in the city follows in the tradition of Cervantes's Don and Pancho Sanchez but instead of traveling through the countryside encountering an endless sequence of characters and adventures, city dwellers grapple with the physically overwhelming metropolis as it generates continuous noise and flux that reverberates internally, within the inner subjective realm. Georg Simmel (1905) captures this tension in his analysis of the modern experience where the individual stands at the center of the social universe, more visible and more interesting than the abstract meta-narratives of historical and economic processes. For Simmel, life in the city marks a new mode of human existence. It is where we collide with an unfamiliar external reality that coerces us to look, observe and think differently. Most importantly, it begins a process of redefining what we may have thought of as natural desires and impulses into conventions and protocols that promise to advantage us in all our social dealings.

Societies are described as being capable of producing identifiable archetypes. In the postmodern societies of the enthusiastic consumer, we are depicted as lamenting the loss of a "true self" and its replacement by a repertoire of calculated maneuvers. We are increasingly familiar with the narrative of the self as an assemblage, and accept the logic that we can be cool hybrid performers who dine out at night in stylish designer rags and then wake up the next day to the drudgery of selling household groceries in a nondescript supermarket. We have formulated a language and conceptual apparatus that makes sense of such metro scripts. In the crowded streets of the twenty-first-century city where we constantly encounter strangers, we have developed modes of operational thinking and acting that emphasize living in the moment. From the background noise, we have extracted a sense of ourselves as coherent entities capable of deriving assurance from the endless offerings of the consumer age (Rorty 1989). Thus, the fashioned body has become a component of human happiness (Thomas 2009: 228). As we struggle towards this perfect state, we learn the value of engaging with scripted social performances made available through popular culture. Our dexterity with the performance of these well-known social scripts keeps us aware of the need to disport ourselves to best effect in every circumstance.

Even as we recognize that our abilities to dissemble and perform are necessary, we also know that deliberating on how to act can seem too calculating and possibly deceptive, as Castiglione warned five hundred years earlier. We know that unless we appear to be spontaneous and sincere, we can easily appear the opposite – unconvincing. As we think twice, three times and more about how to perform socially, we are intuitively drawing on what Roland Barthes referred to as "natural knowledge". This body of knowledge is the taken-for-granted tacit understandings we have absorbed as specific rules of engagement. In our effective performance of these conventions, we appear to others as recognizable characters, even stereotypes. Thus, we meet their expectations and abide by the tacit injunction that being sociable is Castiglione's art of being natural, the "art of being artless".

As we consider the history of manners around self-fashioning and the ways we learn to act in hot and cold environments, it becomes apparent that the restaurant was and continues to be a training ground for the cultivation of the rules of appropriate social engagement.

THE CITY AND MODERN IDENTITY

In the city, we encounter the stranger and we need to be prepared for the unexpected. This proximity to others requires vigilance and a willingness to be adaptive and psychologically alert. Such a perspective is relatively recent and has emerged with the consumer society, where the boundaries between the real and hyperreal, between the actual and imagined, between the obdurate and fleeting, have become much harder to stabilize. The experience of living amid a crowd of strangers trains us to interrogate ourselves. Thus we arrive at a narrative point where ideas about the city and identity begin to overlap with one another and provide a background against which instances of the emotional self become a public text, a performance to be watched, reviewed and we hope sometimes applauded by the anonymous other, especially if it follows the recognizable conventions of the status quo.

The city is the arena in which social ties that had previously bound individuals into self-supporting communities have been loosened, and where new techniques for managing the unanticipated need to be acquired. As the mordant critic of mass culture Theodor Adorno (1981: 262) has said of the city, it is where "the boundary between what is human and the world of things becomes blurred". While the city is not a new configuration, it is now much more than a colossal sculptural installation of buildings and passageways; it is experienced as an arena in which we are constantly on display and as a result on the alert. The celebrated Greek polis of the fifth-century BC was distinctly different from Simmel's modern metropolis. The polis was praised in Pericles's famous oration over the dead as a place that justified personal sacrifice; the city was the pinnacle of human endeavor, it was where humanity demonstrated its better qualities of generosity, inclusiveness and acceptance. In the polis of ancient Athens, the stranger was welcomed and provided with the freedom to enjoy its spectacles and engage in its cosmopolitan practices such as trade and public debate.

By the eighteenth century in the West, the city provided a different backdrop to the individual in search of a social home. By this time, the traditional ways of feudal and rural life had rapidly changed. Almost all of the important European social philosophers of the time were concerned with the changes to mentality that these large-scale social upheavals would bring. They all recognized that the growth of capitalism, industrialization and urbanization would profoundly alter social relationships. Ferdinand Töennies wrote in 1887, in *Gemeinschaft und Gesellschaft*, about the opposed cultures between the provinces and the city. The term *Gemeinschaft* referred to a type of community based on associations of mutual aid and trust. *Gesellschaft* referred to the more urban society characterized by instrumental exchanges based on individual self-interest. In the city, with the congregation of the urban masses, a new fear developed of the anonymous crowd. Individuals were no longer members of a tight community; rather, they could coalesce into a mob and rise up to threaten the established order. The rupture of ties to village, family, church and guild was the "dark side" of the industrial revolution that posed the ever-present possibility of instability.

In concert with these cultural changes, the actual physical world was becoming more crowded with people as well as ideas. Between 1860 and 1910, the population of Simmel's Berlin rose from under half a million people to more than 2 million; Paris increased to nearly 3 million, London from under 3 million to over 4 million, and Vienna from a population less than 1 million in 1869 to almost

2 million in 1910 (Le Rider 1993). The sudden growth of the city as a physical form made it a crucible in which transformations of human experience took shape, often driving the individual toward "the wild pursuit of competition" (Simmel 1900). Everyday encounters were inevitably filled with challenges from other people who looked different, and whose culture, religion, values and aspirations were highly varied. In such circumstances, society became like "a huge arithmetical problem" in which the individual needed to be increasingly calculative (Simmel 1900). The orderliness and regulations of the city, such as timetables for public transport and the regular work hours for factories and shops, produced a sense of stability. Yet this orderliness could easily shatter with chance events such as traffic accidents, mechanical failures and unexpected social encounters. Such consequences gave further support to the anxiety that the social order itself was fragile.

The city was the site of adventure and misadventure. Its romance and allure resided in what might happen; the individual was increasingly aware that opportunities were always unfolding and routines could easily be set aside. Charles Baudelaire, often referred to as the poet of modern capitalism, described the city as a panorama through which the *flâneur*, the quintessential figure of modernity, could wander at will and encounter by chance the spectacular events that the city harbored.

A city is almost always in the throes of transformation, seething with both opportunities and vices. It has been described as an "epicentre for hustlers, bawds, pimps and whores alike (where) a gentleman was just as likely to have his pocket picked as to have his lusts gratified" (Peakman 2004: 2–3). William Hogarth painted many of the more debauched and lascivious antics of Londoners in a city where estimates of the numbers of prostitutes and pimps who made a living from sexual services were as high as 2 percent of the city's population. In every alehouse, there was a backroom set aside for sexual transactions, and the number of brothels, molly-houses and specialist bagnios was well into the hundreds (see http://www.arthistoryspot.com/wp-content/uploads/2010/01/william_hogarth.jpg).

Life in the city has commonly been associated with danger. Simmel highlighted the incipient disorganization of industrial capitalism when he noted that the physical scale of the city, with its plethora of entertainments, corruptions and rank diversions, created a cacophony of noise that literally swept the individual into a moral and aesthetic vertigo. Within such a charged atmosphere, the individual was always in danger of being overwhelmed. To anchor themselves, individuals could grab at visible markers such as material possessions and use them as expressions of personal status and character. Yet this habit too turned out to be unreliable.

The rapid production of goods increased confusion over their value. Using possessions to display position and taste was thus not always convincing. City dwellers needed to learn a language and method for reading their surrounds and for interpreting fashionable dress, physiognomy and speech style as if they were reliable clues to the identity of all they encountered. Being able to decode the character and intentions of the stranger from their outward appearance was marketed as a necessary social skill. Popular crazes for phrenology and palmistry became valued commodities (Sennett 1976). Instruction manuals and primers on how to "read the stranger" became best-sellers. Cheap pamphlets on graphology and quasi-scientific disquisitions on the relationship between body shape and moral character were easily obtained, and there developed a vast market of cranky guides to person-spotting as the best method to grapple with the complexities of urban sociability.

Yet this heightened attention to analyzing and assessing the character of the city-dweller had the ironic effect of creating a disturbing sense of interior emptiness, as if there was a vacuum at the center of the individual's being. The daily habits of association, which required the exercise of indifference, also produced in the individual a repertoire of defense mechanisms that appeared as forms of coolness and reserve. The successful city-dweller was constantly oscillating between a "secret restlessness" and sense of helplessness that was just "below the threshold of consciousness" (Simmel 1900: 484). These opposing mannerisms held the individual and the urban society together in a tangle of mutual demands created by new modes of sociality. They reinforced a sense of interior emptiness sustained by the fleeting revelations from what Walter Benjamin would call dead data: the sounds, scraps and loose gestures of the milling, moving crowd (Benjamin 1982: 525).

The idea of possessing a stable core has popular currency, but so too does the idea that we are capable of self-invention. The inconsistencies and endless permutations that city life produces exist alongside a cherished ideal of an inner coherency. This ambivalence marks an important feature of modernity; namely, the value given to psychology and in particular to the capacity to convert private experiences into effective social roles. The consumer ethic produces an array of identities from which we can select a persona, and popular entertainments in turn reinforce these as attractive models. We become accustomed to thinking of ourselves as characters in an elaborate narrative, a kind of evolving autobiography in which new facets of ourselves are continually taking form and shape. Sometimes, we find ourselves at odds with a situation; we might have misinterpreted the scene and as a result we experience a fractured consciousness that in turn seems to be a kind of psychological misfiring. We explain these social breakdowns as personal maladies rather than a feature of a dislocated or anomic culture where the rules and goals do not jive. The experience of doubt and discomfort can drive us to think again about our capabilities and defects. We imagine we lack some necessary attributes.

This sense of being constantly under construction fits well with the consumer culture that sells identity with most commodities. A stable, coherent self-identity is experienced even though it is constructed from a continuous process of reinvention and adaptation to shifting circumstances. The self thus becomes a target for the merchandizing of an endless array of goods and services. Commodities are advertised through a vocabulary of self-discovery and we have become accustomed to the promises inherent in emotional capitalism (Illouz 2007: 108). The unleashed impulses of the erotic imagination have been replaced by the engineered tastes and values advertised in readily available entertainments.

THE QUEST

In postmodern discourse, the natural subject has been replaced in the materialist West with the quest for an identity that is fluid and adaptive. As we disassemble and reconstruct ourselves, using the ideas about identity that are currently in circulation, we can style ourselves after fashionable character types often found in popular texts. The role of the celebrity musician, athlete, film star, chef and so on provides a template for self-identification. We gain a sense of realism and reality from an all-engrossing entertainment media that promises to reveal the inner secrets, scandals and flaws in all manner of situations from corporate elite culture and the underworld of power in our civic institutions to gritty street life. Particular genres of entertainment are especially popular; namely, the so-called reality programs that have captured more than half of primetime network television. These programs depict a wide variety of situations including family life, middle-class courtship practices, entrepreneurship (*Sylvania Waters*, 1992 Australia; *The 1900 House*, 1999 UK; *Farmer wants a Wife*, 2001 UK; *The Restaurant*, 2003 USA). They also take us behind the scenes in particular workplaces such as emergency rooms in hospitals, customs control offices at international borders, training sessions for extreme sports, and the lifestyles of individuals with unusual bodies such as being the tallest, heaviest, oldest, or shortest person on the planet. Some of the most popular reality television programs are those that show physical makeovers and surgical procedures that alter appearances (*The Swan*, 2004 USA) or where immersion in an environment such as living with strangers requires giving up a normal life (*Castaway*, 2000 UK; *Big Brother*, 2000 UK; *Ladette to Lady*, 2005 UK; *The Apprentice*, 2005 UK). The huge popularity of these programs suggests a widespread cultural value attached to personal transformation, to accepting the idea that identity can be altered and improved by following the example of admired social scripts.

There is also an element of *schadenfreude* in this cultural phenomenon, of taking some pleasure from observing the misfortune of others, and by implication seeing oneself as outside or beyond the same humiliating experience (*Candid Camera*, 1948 USA). The Susan Boyle episode illustrated the fine line that separates visible failure from social success; she has been re-made into a more respectable persona that has distanced her from the embarrassment of that initial television appearance. The plasticity of her appearance reminds us of the possibilities to re-make ourselves. The success of YouTube extends this perspective by providing the technology for re-casting ourselves whenever we wish. It is now within easy grasp that we can represent ourselves in a multiplicity of guises and, indeed, this homemade endorsement of self-invention has become a daily source of entertainment for a global audience (see http://www.youtube.com/watch?v=dRUS5VfkJls&feature= player_embedded).

As techniques for inventing selfhood appear to be increasingly common and accessible, the idea of identity itself seems to be losing some of its intellectual power. It has previously been useful for annotating the lives of individuals who have suffered severe social dislocation such as rapid economic transformation, migration, downward mobility and displacement. The broken, traumatized, collapsed self is the recognizable result. We have entered the interior of the poorly paid shop clerk, nurse, doctor, chef, police officer, prostitute, migrant and so on, as explored through documentary film, reality television and investigative journalism. To some extent, these studies of both damaged and exceptional individuals have made the plasticity of identity even more familiar, and we are increasingly aware that contemporary social life requires pragmatic solutions and continuous adjustment to changing circumstances.

The moving present, the liquid modern, has made the idea of a stable, enduring self seem anachronistic (Bauman 2004: 27). But even with this recognition, the concept of the self continues to be addressed as real. Elements of the personal are in debt to structures of the public, as Charles Horton Cooley described in the early stages of the American sociological enterprise; thus it follows that "a separate individual is an abstraction unknown to experience, and so likewise is society when regarded as something apart from individuals" (1902: 36). We are accustomed to thinking of ourselves as social beings, as agents who make the social world: what is privately and emotionally valued is also part of the normative social frame. However, connecting the social and the private so closely makes them into a single side of a continuously twisting Möbius strip; any distance that might exist between the inside and outside seems to have collapsed. In this way, it is much harder to separate the private experiences of pleasure from public expressions of power that include the power to consume, appropriate and display to others.

The nature of this continuous and intertwined connection between the private and public raises doubts about how much of our private life is fashioned and introjected, how much is formed through individual resistance and self-scrutiny, how balanced is the interplay between our sense of autonomy and the pressures of social conformity. Many of the seemingly banal events of everyday life, such as dining out, illustrate how historical and economic structures become inserted into human imagination. These ordinary events play a part in the manufacture of the private and personal, and beg the question of how much the public character is a magnified version of the private one and vice versa.

At first glance, this position may seem to overburden simple actions with too much symbolic importance. But we need only consider the slippage of the private realm into the public to realize how closely they are intertwined. It is now acceptable to speak on a mobile phone in public, dine out in restaurants, sleep on the bus, walk on the wild side. It may seem an extravagant claim to suggest that a simple gesture can reveal a great deal about a society, but situations penetrate deeply into human consciousness. Gestures and habits of conduct can be indicative of cultural codes and sensibilities. Deliberate gestures seem expressive: a smile, handshake, and wink all convey meaning, although what they mean in a particular context is not always clear. Goffman (1969) describes those impressions that are inadvertently given off and which can discredit the individual and raise doubts about character. The body is constantly expressive; it transmits information all the time, whether intended or not, and some gestures and movements carry long-lasting impressions. The celebrated sex scene in Bernardo Bertolucci's Last Tango in Paris (1972) is retrospectively identified as the explosive moment of ignition of the sexual revolution in the twentieth century; yet acts of this kind, which have circulated through the history of pornography, have been going on for all time (Hunt 1993). Bertolucci captured a moment. There are other tipping points: when did it become acceptable for women and men to shake hands as a form of polite greeting? When did kissing in public become commonplace? When did lighter clothing and the exposure of flesh become attractive? And what of cinematic depictions of sex and violence?

The history of the body and its gestural movements is also a record of social manners. There are well-known accounts of how to read the body such as that provided by Johann Caspar Lavater and Charles Darwin who both attempted to classify universal expressions such as hostility, dominance, happiness and so on. Popular entertainments such as film and television also give definition to practices that are regarded as acceptable and valuable. The capacity of popular culture to disseminate values and social scripts locates it at the center of everyday life where we accept its influence as legitimate. With this authority, popular culture can prescribe everyday practices – hence it explains how the dance style of Michael Jackson infused itself through youth cultures across the globe, and how Bob Dylan became a prophet, and how Alfred Hitchcock intensified the battle of the sexes in mid-America. Unless we accept that "the truth is out there" and not inside, we cannot comprehend how a handshake or a kiss between a man and woman in the twenty-first century would be an unrecognizable gesture in another time and place. Such changes record new habits of living (Bremmer and Roodenburg 1991). In every social act, we transform the "made-up" apprehended world into a world that is "made-real", that seems sensible to us. Every gesture reflects a world beneath the visible exterior; every act is a sign that draws connections between the material and imagined.

THE COLD PRESENT

The shifting fashions in the status of goods are immediately understandable as part of the cyclical and constant circulation of meanings, and this has the effect of creating an insistent level of almost subliminal turbulence in the way we see the world. As we shift our tastes and purchase new wardrobes of varying styles in clothing, and change our musical tastes, and savor one cuisine after another, as we extend our social networks, replace friends and partners and cultivate fresh associations, we are continuously redefining our performance against a shifting, liquid background. Gestures and actions are polysemous and take their meaning from the context. How we choose to behave and conduct ourselves in private and public creates a constant sense of flux as we position ourselves in an external environment rich in choice, that stretches our imagination with its vast array of options to be pursued in the satisfaction of our needs and desires. While we might like the idea that our possessions do define us, that our fashioned appetites insert us – at least for a time – into a prestigious neo-tribe or two that makes us instantly recognizable to ourselves and others, it is also the case that the overwhelming variety of opportunities available to us means that every choice carries some anxiety. The search for distinction is also a constant search for stability in a social milieu that continuously spirals around axes of plenitude. The everyday encounter with abundance and the requirements to make choices produce a crisis of belonging: abundance sets us adrift, we become deterritorialized, made déclassé, without social hinges that are elsewhere promised to give a sense of community. In its stead, there are the virtual communities of reality television, social networking through Facebook and the tribal affiliations of branded products.

The quest for self-knowledge and identity emerges from the new ways in which we have learned to be introspective and private. Modern living has required us to submerge certain of our appetites and emotions into more mannered modes of conduct. These modes of living in the world become part of deeply encoded frameworks of meaning that correspond to well-recognized public conventions. In *Mythologies* (1972), Roland Barthes described this as a form of "natural knowledge" that is actually a fabrication, a mythology. He described how ideas seem self-evidently true, as if they were eternal facts, when they are better understood as anthems of a particular socio-political regime. We are familiar with contemporary values that suggest ways we should live and the ideas we should believe – such as freedom is possible, money is power, greed is good, love conquers all, feelings are to be trusted, appearances matter, everyone lies and so on. Such ideas have currency and they form the lexicon of everyday culture. Our familiarity with them lends them authority. Yet Barthes warns, at this point, that if we are to be autonomous, self-fashioning and responsible social members, we need to denaturalize these taken-for-granted truisms and uncover the social and political frameworks they assume. Barthes has argued that unless we understand how natural knowledge comes into being and how deeply enculturated it is, we cannot consider ourselves autonomous enough to have a moral system or an independent point of view.

Every social act is framed within the norms of the circumstance. The struggle to give an account of the nature of social life and how we should live draws on a long history of speculation about how meanings have been produced and made to seem natural. The idea of individualism itself is sanctioned by a multitude of everyday customs that repeatedly make it meaningful. Advertising addresses us – *Just Do It, Keep Calm and Carry On, Uncle Sam Needs You, We do it all for you.* How such ideas work, and the mechanisms supporting their social diffusion and acceptance, entails a close study of everyday forms.

In this way, a narrow focus on the popularity of dining out in the cold restaurant identifies it as a social carrier of familiar ideas about identity. As long as dining out is seen as a convenience, as a shared pleasure between friends and family, it will appear entirely benign. However, the history of the restaurant demonstrates that it has been and continues to be a more contested space. The modern industrialization of food and the part it plays in the expanding entertainment and leisure industries gives it further social, economic and political significance. The restaurant contributes ideas and practices into the wider symbolic economy. It is an exhibition space where signs of social mobility and status are demonstrated, where exchanges of disjunctive social forces are exposed, where personal expressions of self-promotion and self-delusion are enacted. As such, it is a micro-spectacle of the society at large.

In the restaurant, a great deal of attention is paid to the style of the performance; it is an environment where a high degree of watchfulness takes place. This attention to the nature of action makes it an engineered and cold environment. In contrast, a sports crowd, in which the individual is anonymous and thereby free to make spontaneous outbursts of enthusiasm and express impulsive emotions, can be described as a hot environment. Such situations are less predictable and more eruptive. The cinema and sports field are both designed to generate an engaged mob, as Gustave Le Bon (1896) suggested more than a century ago in his study of *The Crowd*, but that entity itself is not a single, stable category: mobs, crowds, audiences and teams are not all alike, even when they are happy and triumphant. In all social situations, there is a continual exchange between the physical setting and the conduct of the individual that is reflected in the hot and cold temperature of the situation and in the semiotic details of the circumstances themselves. Once we choose the type of restaurant we want for a particular occasion, we can expect to feel secure in the experience it delivers. A busy restaurant, unlike a football crowd, successfully engineers the expression of fashionable values and lifestyles currently in circulation. Its pleasures are in its consistent meeting of our expectations and this makes the coldness of the restaurant its popular attraction.

Social spaces elicit certain behavior, even though they cannot always predict and control the outcomes. Some situations can be described as hot and unpredictable, others as cold and controlled. The restaurant is the latter. Whether it is formal or casual, expensive or cheap, celebrated or suburban, it frames the experience. This is managed through the service provided, the cost of the comestibles, the speed of the meal, the design of the social space, the quality of the decor. The average length of time in a fast food outlet is much shorter than in a bistro mondain; the self-service style of the fast food outlet frames the experience in a more structured and predictable way than the service provided by a waiter. Nonetheless, the commonality linking all restaurants is their level of engineering and containment. The differences in temperature between a hot and cold situation rest on the intensity of the participants and their sense of personal engagement. Cold environments have legacies that hot environments do not; cold environments are more stable and have institutional memories that hot environments lack. In a hot environment, a large sports gathering (football, cricket, horse-racing), the tempo of the situation is determined by the competitive performances of the athletes (human or animal). In contrast, a restaurant has a reputation; it has an establishment of personnel that are trained to be consistent in their delivery; it is deliberate in its orchestration of a specific outcome − namely, a type of pleasurable experience that must remain the same over an extended period of time.

How we act in public, and how we know what is important, emerges from an engagement with social institutions such as the restaurant that bestows author- ity on certain ways of living. The consumer culture, in particular, encourages the mixture of food with sociability and emotional satisfaction, and as a result the commercial success of the restaurant has compressed the expression of private emotions into the activities of public capital. This makes the restaurant an influential element in the formation of modern identity. Irrespective of the type of restaurant in which we eat, the environment is always engineered. The history of the restaurant tracks its evolution from the bawdy coffeehouse into a disciplinary arena in which private pleasures are defined and contained within the protocols of the public space.

6 THE BANALITY OF FOOD

Taste governs every free – as opposed to rote – human response. Nothing is more decisive. There is taste in people, visual taste, taste in emotion – and there is taste in acts, taste in morality. Intelligence, as well, is a kind of taste: taste in ideas.

SUSAN SONTAG

The range of restaurants, cafés and commercial eating places has increased dramatically over the past fifty years. Almost everyone at some time or another has eaten out. The trend in the UK shows that about one-third of all meals are purchased and consumed outside the home, in public, in a café, pub or restaurant (Burnett 2004: 291). In the USA, about 50 percent of every food dollar is spent on purchases consumed outside the home (Trubek 2007: 35, quoting the 2003 National Restaurant Association). The centrality of the restaurant itself remains important in shaping contemporary public life. Restaurants in all their diversity reflect characteristics of their patrons; they are in the business of providing pleasure and the specific emotional satisfactions that accompany its pursuit. Whether it is dining *à la mode* or in the local fast food outlet, the restaurant is a highly engineered setting and we have agreed to abide by its tacit rules.

Coffee houses, the presumed ancestor of the restaurant, were noted to exist as early as 1560 in Constantinople and they proliferated throughout most European cities from the mid-seventeenth century. In London, they were known as "tattling universities", a description that alluded to the chaotic mix of social classes that mingled there as well as the busy exchanges of ideas that took place over a drink of the new sensation, coffee. In this social space, traders, landed gentry, aristocrats, louches and the new urban professionals were free to speak to one another across the otherwise constraining barriers of class and status. Such establishments also provided shelter to those who traded on the street such as prostitutes, petty criminals and thieves (Trumbach 1987: 80).

The early restaurant provided a social space where experimenting with one's capacities for observation and analysis became an important social skill. The fashionable urban culture of the eighteenth century encouraged subterfuge as disguised individuals used the anonymous street to procure a variety of novel sensations. Terry Castle (1987: 157) cites Boswell's journals where on occasion, when dressed as a soldier or a low-life ruffian, he would seek clandestine sexual adventures. It was widely understood that appearances could be misleading and disguises were popular; thus it was possible to misread the stranger and fail to understand the significance of certain bodily signs. The stranger always posed a threat. However, if gestures and bodily signs could be better read, if there was a prescriptive formula for interpreting them as promised by physiognomic reasoning, then the social encounter would become more predictable and less dangerous. The restaurant, as part of the newly opened public space, became a place where mutual scrutiny was encouraged and where the individual could cultivate their capacities for observation and skilful reading of the other. The restaurant was a laboratory where tastes, no matter how fleeting, were exposed and indulged and where novel social experiences were manufactured (Gronow 1997). In the restaurant, the individual was made more visible.

Early traders learned that customers were attracted by the entertainments and distractions on offer in the coffee house, especially the opportunities to seek transgressive pleasures and secret assignations. Such features made the restaurant into a pleasure dome, an escape from ordinary, everyday concerns. The offer of private spaces outside the domestic home came first in the form of separate tables (in contrast to the long, communal table at a travelers' inn) and then in private rooms or cabinets that held just a few people. This desire for privacy and anonymity while in a crowd influenced the architecture of the restaurant with its provision of separate spaces. The restaurant then became a fashionable venue for pursuing unconstrained intimacies in the public domain and allowed escapades into new sensual and ethical underworlds.

The various carnivals, festivals and the scandalous masquerade balls such as those held in the Haymarket Theatre in London provided venues for talk, conversation, gossip, and the spread of news and views. These social meeting places were the chief means for transmitting information about fashions and entertainments. As Thomas (2009: 223) reports: "gossip was not a trivial matter. It afforded pleasure to connoisseurs of narrative detail and human idiosyncrasy... (it was) one of humanity's defining characteristics... conversation was an end in itself". The historian of the restaurant, Rebecca Spang (2000: 3–5), described it as a site where the eighteenth-century sensibility focused on health and vigor slowly evolved into the nineteenth-century emphasis on the cultivation of good taste. It was in these fashionable practices that new social forms and subjectivities were being shaped alongside other pastimes such as gourmandizing. The restaurant was feeding and entertaining people as well as providing a setting for unfettered socializing and endless talk. Against this background, individualism and its associated sensibilities were being emphasized: "restaurant service was reserved for, defined by, and perhaps instrumental in creating, individuals" (Spang 2000: 75).

The several hundred years over which the modern restaurant evolved cover a corresponding period of cultural history in which the contemporary emphasis on psychological reasoning and the presentation of the self can be seen to have developed through a wide net of interconnected social processes. The restaurant is an engineered space, irrespective of whether it is the self-servicing fast food outlet or the silver service of the *Fête Spéciale*, and as such it promotes conformity. How we have acquired the necessary attributes to act in such circumstances emerges from a long history of early mercantilism and the growth of the city itself. The new open public sphere and the changing nature of sociality are well illustrated in the coffee house where experiments took place in talking across the social barriers. In the coffee house, individuals learned new ways to see and think about themselves and others. They were schools of subjectivity.

The early restaurant was also a theater for spectacle, a place where the unexpected was welcomed. Its tolerance of the bawdy, lascivious, transgressive and boisterous meant that individuals learned to become increasingly tolerant of others and prepared to indulge their peculiarities. These social arenas put the individual on display; people could linger and be entertained by observing others as well as being a source of amusement themselves. The public domain became a stage for experimentation. Individuals were openly studied; the details of their dress and deportment were decipherable signs of their status and proclivities. Styled appearances made the manners of dissemblance more obvious. In these ways, the perception takes hold that the social world is a theater where all human relations are continuously staged and engineered and this marks the beginning of what are now familiar styles and conventions.

From these forerunners, we have learned the importance of how others see us. How we disport ourselves and indulge in voluntary acts of consumption and entertainment give visible form to our tastes and pleasures. That means every gesture and action is a display of our aesthetic and ethical views on the world and, according to Cooley, Elias, Bourdieu, Barthes and others, it cannot be otherwise. This is the machinery of the civilizing process. By engaging with strangers, by being in the same social space with them and by interacting in more complex encounters through trade and conversation, we place ourselves in a position of having to accept how they see us and, further, of understanding their point of view when it may not accord with our own. In every transaction, there are opportunities for misunderstandings. To bridge these potential differences, we promote a shared language and set of values attached to specific activities. Hence objects become branded with cultural values and fashions are used to convey defining attributes – for instance, age, class and gender. A rudimentary system of mutually understood practices emerges around popular objects and practices.

This is well illustrated by the engineered atmosphere of the restaurant, where the mannered event of dining out has been superimposed on our quest for happiness and fulfilment, where the decor and artifice of the place have been designed to produce an emotional response, where customs locate us in a framework of prefigured satisfactions. In the restaurant, we expect to feel certain sensations such as security and amiability; we have learned to dine out in order to seek reassurance and a sense of social acceptability; that we belong, that we are in fashion. This is emotional capitalism in action; all the familiar habits of the everyday have been invested with meaning; every object, event and encounter can be measured in terms of emotional dividends. We assume we know what it means to own a Ferrari, go nightclubbing, wear Brooks Brothers, attend the annual Bayreuth Festival or to dine at The Wolseley and Michael Mina. As a result of the emotional investments made in these objects and activities, society is dominated by a trade in certain pleasures. The everyday is awash with desires and fantasies that supposedly hinge to specific events and practices. We know what to feel, see and expect at a shopping mall, open-air rock concert, up-market deli and Michelin-starred restaurant. An emotional repertoire is regularly played out through our consumer practices including the pleasure we find in popular entertainments such as dining out.

COLD RESTAURANTS

From the boisterous liberalism of eighteenth-century street life to the engineered pursuit of desires in the twenty-first century, there is a visible trend of increased reserve and containment in our styles of interaction. We have learned to curb our physical impulses in order to indulge our consumer desires. We have become more self-conscious and controlled in our mannerisms as we imagine we are being more closely observed by others. Ironically, this intensified self-scrutiny becomes the best means for expressing our desires. Scholars of human gestures, such as Norbert Elias (1978), Michel Foucault (1978), Clifford Geertz (1983) and Erving Goffman (1961) have persuasively established links between individual mannerisms of the body and broader collective sensibilities. The behavioral norms surrounding how we eat, as we have seen, transmit cultural knowledge, and the increasing popularity of dining out connects the particularities of individual tastes and social habits with a history in which appetites and passions have been associated with class, gender and education. The business of learning how to communicate, to express and convey ideas and feelings, is intrinsic to becoming cosmopolitan. Both Georg Simmel and Norbert Elias have separately described the distinctive mien that social actors need to cultivate in order to succeed socially. The *blasé* attitude, described by Simmel, was essential to living in the crowded, noisy city and the heightened thresholds of tolerance described by Elias have enabled us to display polite civility in the face of differences and provocations from strangers. Embedded in these cultural practices is a recognition that we need to have a sharper awareness of one another in order to pursue our own interests.

The slow regimentation of social exchange through the dissemination of guidebooks and instructional manuals marks a further stage in the cooling process that brings into existence the orderly and ritualized manners now found in modern institutions like the restaurant. Official guidebooks to the world at large aid this process and have been a comforting possession of the middle classes since the mid-nineteenth century. Guidebooks provide a wide range of advice depending on their audience; some suggest travel routes and give the best prices of hotels and restaurants, and even offer an opinion on the grandeur or not of the passing scenery. The extensive use made of the Baedeker for travel in Europe was promoted by the travel company Thomas Cook and famously mentioned in E.M. Forster's *A Room with a View*. Other forms of instructional literature are couched as life-changing adventures such as Vikram Seth (1987), *From Heaven Lake*, Peter Mayle (1990), *A Year in Provence*, or Ros Pesman (1996), *Duty Free*. Expert guidebooks have been very popular with the middle classes who have made extensive use of them in all aspects of their lives: Dale Carnegie (1936) on making friends and influencing people; Dr Spock (1946) on raising babies; Steven Covey (1989) on business success; Richard Florida (2002) on creativity. In searching for good advice, food has been no exception; where to eat and why have been the basis of a range of guidebooks such as *Cheap Eats*, *Lonely Planet*, *Rough Guide*, *The Good Food Guide* and *Gayot* as well as more established and prestigious advice found in the *Michelin Red Book* and *Gault Millau*.

The need for advice about lifestyle choices corresponds with patterns of social mobility and the existence of a more crowded marketplace where the number of goods and choices available to consumers has increased. As more products with similar features become available, consumers themselves become the target for market differentiation. Products become personalized: all manner of goods become imbued with characteristics and attributes that address the personal values of the consumer, thereby making the purchase into a mode of self-display. Motor cars, perfume, sofas, cutlery, pet food, breakfast cereals and so on have gained market presence by displaying attractive attributes that resonate with the values and lifestyles of those who use them. Types of food and the manner of consumption reflect similar merchandizing techniques. Consumer choice is notoriously difficult to predict, yet changes to the marketplace itself create circumstances in which choices appear to be patterned

(Wood 1995). For instance, the expression of region and heritage has now been inserted into many food products. We like to know where the cheese, pasta, virgin oil and wine have been sourced. This interest has been applied as a marketing strategy as it complements a more diffuse interest in searching for heritage and "roots". In an era of high mobility and social hybridity, a sense of community, location and family have thus become more acute as implied by the popularity of DIY family trees and reality television programs that ask "who are you and where did you come from?". The restaurant and the contemporary habit of dining out form part of this quest for identity and position by offering to materialize and display personal qualities and tastes to a world we imagine is interested.

LIFE AT THE SURFACE

The changes in cultural habits across several centuries of social and commercial development are not linear or logical, but are illustrative of the connections between the most trivial gestures and the insertion of cultural habits into individual consciousness. The physiognomic system of observation popularized by Johann Caspar Lavater in the eighteenth century has been repeated many times in subsequent literature, not because of its accuracy in analyzing character but, more generally, as a result of the emphasis it brought to the value of reading details. It is difficult to provide all the links that chain together meanings from one set of actions to another but, in descriptions of our tastes — for a cup of coffee bought from a global outlet such as Starbucks or from a local espresso bar, or for shopping at a farmers' market in preference to a generic supermarket — there can be seen other related practices that exist alongside. Tastes are closely associated with external circumstances and with individual status and self-identification as illustrated by Bourdieu's mapping of distinctions. These interconnections demonstrate the strong association and reciprocity that ties together the personal and the social. These connections, however, are not static but need to be constantly reinforced with repeated practice. Such regularity makes them seem more natural than they are and more conventional. This is the re-enactment of the disciplined society and the mythologies of the natural world that both Foucault and Barthes have separately identified.

In Michel de Certeau's (1984) analysis of everyday life, he produces "a science of singularity" in which everyday pursuits are again linked to circumstances. It is in the details of daily transactions that we learn how to express autonomy and establish viable social relations within a grid of socio-economic constraints. The assumption is that the everyday world is not a private universe but is formulated in relation to others. As we purchase entertainments from a dizzying array of goods and services, we may consider ourselves free, autonomous beings, but for Certeau (1984: ix–xii) we are not such singular creatures. He describes us as "poachers" who constantly appropriate from others in order to sustain ourselves. The emotional investments we make in ordinary practices reveal assumptions about the nature of society and Certeau identifies commercial influences from advertising, fashion, the broadcast of information and popular entertainments as being the strongest forces in its formulation (Certaeu: 180–5).

Definitions of the real and the valuable are constantly circulated through popular media, and the more they are discussed, the more likely they are to infuse prevailing attitudes and views. In effect, as we become increasingly proficient with fashions and conventions, we become more deeply and perhaps complacently inserted into recognizable patterns and practices; as a result, it becomes harder to see their arbitrariness or any reason to challenge and change them. The consumerist culture, with its comprehensive network of communications and promotion of the illusory world of advertised images, has come to prefabricate much of everyday social life. Cultural values are sold at every opportunity. This does not always happen in obvious ways, but more commonly it infiltrates our everyday habits through casual and irresistible encounters that subsequently reverberate through our thoughts and feelings. We do not simply absorb a singular image or set of ideas from external sources – we construct narratives around these encounters and re-frame them into more enduring ideas that function to explain the world and ourselves to ourselves. Thus begins the process by which we become our tastes, and our tastes advertise us, as Henry James's anti-hero Serena Merle states: "I know a large part of myself is in the clothes I choose to wear. I've a great respect for *things!*

In an account of contemporary celebrity, Fred Inglis (2010: 25–31) argues that certain historical epochs cultivate specific emotional responses that in turn reflect how we think of ourselves and others. There is a developmental progression in the circulation of emotions through which we learn how to feel and how to regulate these feelings. We understand intuitively that we possess certain preferences for food, people, objects, music and so on, and these preferences are more than rational choices and distinctions; they are fueled by emotions, by strong feelings. Certain cultures and social groupings promote specific feelings and rank these in a hierarchical system of order (Inglis 2010: 30). As a result, some emotions become entangled with other values; thus we learn to "love" chocolate biscuits, money, physical beauty and individual freedom. Inglis uses the prevalence of reality television programs and the cult of celebrity to show how certain hierarchies become established; he cites, for example, the elevation of chefs in importance over scientists (Inglis: 18). The global popularity of certain entertainments like reality television has the effect of strengthening our allegiance to hyperreality, to the images of the worlds we long to occupy. Popular television and film provide persuasive examples of how certain ideas and fashions percolate across different corners of the globe and come to form connecting discourses that promote particular values. It is a point made by Umberto Eco in his arguments about the prevalence of hyperreality (1986). In a different context, Susan Sontag (1973: 161) has made the same point – the popularity of photography has given emphasis to surface appearances and in so doing has inadvertently redefined the world we think of as real: "reality has come to seem more and more like what we are shown by cameras". It is a position with disturbing consequences: "what is real has been progressively complicated and weakened" (Sontag 1973: 160).

There are myriad examples of the success of the image redefining what we see. The popular *Star Wars* films produced Darth Vader dolls and dress-up costumes for children, and the more recent television series *Mad Men* has generated tie-in products such as nail varnish based on the colors of the women's clothes and Mattel toy dolls in imitation of the show's characters. These are trivial examples, but as they yield substantial economic returns and create a widely used language around such television series, they take on greater social significance. The supposed realism of programs like the long-running *West Wing* raises the question of how representable real social and political life can be in an era saturated with hyperreal depictions. Even when such programs address contemporary social concerns such as the exercise of political power, the use of propaganda, the manipulation of broadcast news, the existence of racism, the effects of financial crisis and personal traumas such as alcoholism, drug addiction, rape and domestic violence, still the representations are being mediated through a lens focused on providing entertainment.

As reality television has become increasingly popular as a form of entertainment, it has been renamed banality television. These programs encompass a wide range of situations from the realistic to the fantastic, from contemptuous of the participants (*The Weakest Link*) to pandering to the audience (*Deal or No Deal*). Many reality television shows are self-referential and stay tightly boxed within an artificial space. This maintains the orderliness of a successful format and prevents any awkward disruptions, but it has the effect of depicting ordinary situations as if they were in reality confined and repetitive. Such programs cut off the participants from the external open society where events do not always follow a formula and where decision-making does not always produce a timely result. This is the key feature that makes reality television unreal, indeed, hyperreal; it is a form of entertainment that deliberately blurs the boundary between the actual and fabricated. Such programs mimic real situations (the home, office, air travel, shopping) but also degrade their significance by trimming off the exceptional and concentrating on the standardized. Other programs emphasize the opposite; that is, they highlight the exceptional and exotic but then domesticate them within the claustrophobic format of the show (*The Jerry Springer Show*; *Larry King Live*; *The Graham Norton Show*). In both extremes, we the audience are taken into the realms of the luminous ideal (what life can offer) and the unhappy real (the circumstances over which we have no control). Not surprisingly, the distinctions between them are blurred, creating in turn an anomic disjuncture between the possible and the improbable.

The popularity of reality television programs is underscored by the diversity of their topics; they include real estate programs that follow the progress of people buying houses (*Location, Location, Location*; *Escape to the Country*; *A Place in the Sun*), travel programs (*Coach Trip*), food programs (*Cookery School*; *Iron Chef*; *Gourmet Farmer*; *Food Network*), difficult occupations (*Grimefighters*; *Junior Doctors*; *Supernanny*), extreme sports (*Gladiators*), consumer education (*Bargain Hunt*; *Flog It!*; *Hotter than my Daughter*) and competitive programs (*The Apprentice*; *Judge Judy*). Despite their diversity, the programs are themselves repetitive, using a similar style of presentation in each of their episodes.

The significance of such popular entertainment is the emphasis it gives to surface appearances. Even when an attempt is made to be exploratory and investigative, the emphasis on the sincerity of the representation buries the subtext. In the new type of reality shows that have developed from the traditions of the documentary film, we are presented with hermetically sealed narratives that promote their own veracity. The contemporary documentaries *Super Size Me* (2004) directed by Morgan Spurlock, and *Catfish* (2010) directed by Ariel Schulman represent the next generation of reality programing. *Super Size Me* (2004) was filmed over a 30-day period in which the director restricted himself to eating all his meals at McDonald's in order to highlight the deleterious effect of fast foods. Spurlock stated that his purpose was to show the dangers in the increasing rates of obesity. He considered fast food to be as physiologically addictive and harmful to health as tobacco smoking. The film recorded the changes to Spurlock's body and mental well-being during his month-long diet. He gained over 10 percent of his original body weight and experienced previously unknown mood swings. The experience was unremittingly negative and even threatened long-term organ damage to his kidneys and liver. Critics of Spurlock's film claimed it was an unreal depiction of the McDonald's food experience and thus failed to achieve its purpose. They argued that very few people follow an exclusive diet of McDonald's and that to spend a month eating only items from the McDonald's menu was a stunt. The project of the film was to bring reality and entertainment close together. Spurlock turned himself into a body artist in the same category as Orlan and Stelarc, making his body into an object for scrutiny, an aesthetic field that deliberately blurred the definitions of the real and performed. The perennial question about such art is pertinent in this case – did *Super Size Me* achieve its aim? Did it change attitudes toward obesity? Did it do more than frame McDonald's once again as a globally recognized, financially successful corporate giant?

Another independent film purporting to explore the hyperreality of social media was *Catfish* (2010), directed by Henry Joost and Ariel Schulman. It narrated the romance of Nev Schulman, the film-maker's younger brother, as he developed a relationship with a woman he met through the social network Facebook. The film documented the relationship from beginning to end, over several months' duration, and revealed the ease with which fabricated lives can be devised through this medium. The young woman of Nev's affections turned out not to exist, and in her place was a married couple with a suburban life largely shaped around the care of two disabled children. The father of the disabled children explains the title of the film, *Catfish*, in the closing sequence: he tells Nev that the world is made up of two kinds of people – those who act like catfish and the others, who resemble cod. The catfish is aggressive and constantly nibbles at the cod, threatening their existence, and subsequently forces them to become more active, more nimble, more aware of the need to be self-protective. The film closes on this homily, warning the audience that it is relatively easy to falsify reality and that all is not what it appears to be. The film is at this point asking to be read as a statement of fact and not an entertainment or a work of art – in which case, does it work? Does it distance us from the real, as art often does in order to question the nature of its subject? In this instance, does it challenge the cultural myth that romantic love is an effective device that mobilizes us, much like the eponymous catfish itself?

In both these examples, the more general problem being illustrated with everyday life televised as art and entertainment is that the surface is being presented as if it were sufficient. Thus, there is no need to know more about the social scene: the film has supposedly captured the full reality. As Sontag (1973: 160) stated: reality seems more like an image of itself. The popularity of this type of entertainment supports an illusion that real life can be and even should be contained within a recognizable format. These entertainments appear to be entertaining diversions that relieve us, at least temporarily, of the necessity to cultivate the manners of thinking that better equip us for everyday life. *The Apprentice*, for instance, a long-running reality television program screened in the UK, Australia and the USA over the past decade, follows the quest of small groups who are paced through a series of challenges before presenting themselves, each week, to be evaluated by three established professionals. The attention lavished on these adventurers exceeds that which is commonly provided in job recruitment; while we might imagine we would enjoy receiving the focused attention of such a high-powered triumvirate, in actuality, it rarely happens. The program works from the popular belief that we will be discovered, that our talents will be recognized and we will be propelled to stardom, much like Susan Boyle.

Such examples are demonstrations of cultural values that we have absorbed, perhaps without noticing, into the repertoires of everyday life. These entertainments provide templates for daily existence, and their popular expressions and imitative gestures readily flow from the television screen to infuse daily habits of social exchange. This one-way flow brings attention to the undercurrents that define and industrialize the emotional economy. If we think again about dining out as an element in the entertainment industries as well as part of the global economy of food manufacture and distribution, marketing and advertising, it brings a sharper focus to the ways in which our tastes can be shaped and colonized. Such a consideration involves a review of the structured and engineered public domain in order to understand how pleasures and amusements are defined according to interests that may be remote from our own. If we succeed in linking activities like dining out more closely to the episodic representations of everyday life that are commonly provided through formulaic entertainments found in reality television programs, then the restaurant may not seem as benign and uncomplicated.

Towards the untimely end of his life, Michel Foucault was considering the care of self by which he drew attention to the nature of our subjectivity, to questions of how we acquire and then follow the dictates of our tastes, and the circumstances in which emotions, desires and proclivities are cultivated. It is this same concern that emerges from consideration of engagement with forms of popular entertainments. Dining out has become a normal event. It seems banal and hence benign; after all, we choose to eat out, we are willing participants and we know what we are doing. The restaurant has the capacity to be a ludic space; it invites us to play by providing comfort, entertainment and in many instances anonymity. In its early form, the restaurant encouraged the liberation of desires by creating opportunities for experimental and casual encounters that crossed various social barriers such as class, gender, politics and religion. Its early European association with health spas and the revitalizing demitasse of bouillon marked the beginning of its commercial character, but it also pointed toward its more theatrical nature that encouraged a burlesque exchange of goods and services.

These characteristics have been modified. Now the restaurant is so widely accepted as a convenience of modern life that it is part of the background, the taken-for-granted overlooked wallpaper. Little critical recognition exists in the mainstream media of its capacity to exert a powerful influence over cultural habits. The collapse of the private into the public extends the network of social control that works effectively through the commercialization of our tastes and appetites. This is the exercise of power not as a negative that suppresses or dominates, but rather as a production of possibilities. The restaurant, like other public performative spaces, provides an operative field of possibilities for the exercise of choice: we know we will enjoy ourselves when in our favorite bistro or celebrated Michelin-starred eatery. In our decision to dine out, we are immediately inserted into an elaborate system of classification of food prescribed through popular culture. By choosing to dine out (or buy a car, take a holiday, select shoes, a frock, a necktie or perfume to purchase), we are immediately categorized, defined, disciplined and normalized. In this case, our eating habits identify us. As Foucault has repeatedly indicated, the sign becomes itself and bears back to reinstate itself. Thus, taste reconstitutes us even as we consider its cultivation to be a means of changing ourselves.

Food is a common and global concern; it provides immediate personal and visceral pleasures and sustains a colossal economic system. Driving the revolution in the food business is the enlarged market of consumers who have aestheticized food and made it into a continuous source of entertainment and novelty. From the longevity of the fashion for haute cuisine to the popularity of cooking programs on television with their companion recipe books and lushly photographed gastro-porn food magazines, the aura around food has transformed it into an industrialized status symbol. We use the restaurant for convenience and in so doing we accept its capacity to trade in tastes. Social distinctions are symbolized through food and these in turn produce a system of ranked preferences; the taste for oysters is ranked above the cheeseburger, and Dom Pérignon above Bud. The display of taste is a form of power – to impose distinctions and values. Changes in culinary styles over 300 years reflect changes in the repertoire of human sociality; the display of tolerance towards others and the use of food to rank and order experience all reveal aspects of the present. The contemporary conventions around food reveal the expansion of the psychological view, of how we have learned to think about others, and how such an interest influences our own self-knowledge. This level of attention shown to the opinions of others supports a form of social life dominated by details, such as the constant comparison of banal habits that function to locate us in the wider social fabric. Our practice of privacy, intimacy and pleasure has thus been superimposed on consumer fashions and we have become the target for a commerce in emotion.

While food and eating are universals and integral to the framework of society, in the West, the popularity of the restaurant has connected such ordinary acts to big business and redefined food as a form of consumable entertainment. The visual history of food has been subsumed into this enterprise: from the ingenuity of Arcimboldo's ludic paintings to the *schadenfreude* moment when Krapp slips on the banana skin in Samuel Beckett's bleak play, food has found a place in the entertainment industries. It is much less about sustenance and much more about status, entertainment, conspicuous consumption and display. It has been absorbed into the reciprocal connections between the fashionability of iconic goods and the display of personal identity.

Restaurants are represented as interesting places that demonstrate varying levels of glamor and aesthetic sophistication: they have celebrated chefs who publish glossy recipe and food books and appear on television. They are part of a globally successful economy that provides a reputable product, good service and reliable financial profit. The food industries have built market demand for their products, for convenient foods that have rapidly changed the meaning of food from a basic form of nutrition into forms of leisure and entertainment to be enjoyed both inside and outside the home. The restaurant industry has simultaneously sustained a strong growth in the mass marketing of standardized foods and produced a consumer interested in food as a convenience and a form of entertainment. Yet this kind of attention somewhat overshadows the social experimentation that has been historically associated with the enlargement of the public domain. As a consequence, it is possible to see how the restaurant, in all its manifestations, is now a much more conservative and structured space in concert with the fine-grained networks of social constraints in which we voluntarily participate.

To enjoy what the restaurant has to offer, we have learned by observation, imitation and practice how to accept the conventions of dining out and follow the rules of the situation. The restaurant engineers circumstances in which personal proclivities can be satisfied and certain emotions produced on the proviso that we assent to the restaurant's protocols. The restaurant brings strangers together to pursue their own private desires within a public space structured to separate us. In the long evolution from the noisy coffee house to the opulent chinoiserie of the China Tang Bar in The Dorchester via the high street café and the global food outlet, the restaurant has paralleled the grooming of the modern individual; it has contributed to the construction of the contemporary cosmopolitan who seeks to enjoy privacy in the public, and balances the rewards of prescribed pleasures with being an atomized, anomic consumer.

The tell-tale details in the way food has come to be presented provide apertures through which we can see the machinery of cultural production itself. Studying culture from the inside requires detachment, a position disavowed of thorough social training. Detachment is necessary – but made difficult by the saturation of everyday life with media images that repeatedly provide hyperbolic versions of social reality. The overlay of hyperreality, the phantasmagoric world of branded goods and designer materials, creates a gap between the material reality and its symbolic form, and re-makes what we understand as the real into an image of itself. It is reputed that Marshall McLuhan, the early critic of the mass media, described the difficulty of explaining the social as being equivalent to explaining the nature of water to a fish (Taylor and Harris 2008: 2). The problem is making the invisible obvious, which is tantamount to treating the obvious as more than it appears. Thus, in this study of the restaurant and how our conduct around food connects to the ways we understand ourselves, it has been the odd, amusing and arresting details such as the idiosyncratic signage on the toilets at the exclusive restaurant Half Moon and the inversion of the appropriated McDonald's advertisement that piques curiosity about how food has been transformed into a commodified entertainment. Our engagement with these seemingly trivial activities works to support an everyday culture that aestheticizes food and occludes the wider context of the global economy of powerful corporations that market fashions and, with them, personal identity.

BIBLIOGRAPHY

Adorno, Theodor (1981). "Notes on Kafka", in *Prisms*, Mass.: MIT.

Akerman, Nordal (1993). *The Necessity of Friction*, New York: Springer-Verlag.

Alexander, Stephanie (2002). *Cooking and Travelling in South-West France*, Melbourne: Penguin.

——— (2012). *A Cook's Life*, Melbourne: Penguin.

Aries, Philipppe (1962). *Centuries of Childhood*, New York: Vintage.

Aristotle (1995). *Politics*, Oxford: Clarendon.

Austen, Jane (1813). *Pride and Prejudice*, Harmonds: Penguin.

——— (1814). *Mansfield Park*, Harmonds: Penguin.

Axe Dark Temptation advert for deodorant using chocolate man, retrieved from: http://www.dailymotion.com/video/x6u7ue_new-axe-dark-temptation-commercial_fun.

Baghurst, Katrine (2007). "Nutritional Recommendations for the General Population", in Jim Mann and Stewart Truswell (eds), *Essentials of Human Nutrition*, Oxford: Oxford University Press.

Baker, Nicholson (1988). *The Mezzanine*, New York: Vintage.

Barthel, Diane (1982). "Modernism and Marketing: The Chocolate Box Revisited", *Theory, Culture & Society* 6: 429–38.

Barthes, Roland (1972). *Mythologies*, London: Jonathan Cape.

——— (1982). *The Empire of Signs*, New York: Farrar, Straus & Giroux.

Bauman, Zygmunt (2001). *The Individualized Society*, Oxford: Polity.

——— (2004). *Identity: Conversations with Benedetto Vecchi*, Oxford: Polity.

Bell, David and Gill Valentine (1997). *Consuming Geographies*, London: Routledge.

Benjamin, Walter (1982). *Gesammelte schriften V: Das Passagen-werk*, Frankfurt: Suhrkamp.

Benstock, Shari (1986). *Women of the Left Bank: Paris 1900–1940*, Austin, TX: University of Texas.

Beriss, David and David Sutton (eds) (2007). *The Restaurants Book: Ethnographies of Where We Eat*, Oxford: Berg.

Berger, Peter L. and Thomas Luckmann (1966). *The Social Construction of Reality*, New York: Doubleday.

Bordo, Susan (2000). "Hunger As Ideology", in Juliet B. Schor and Douglas B. Holt (eds), *The Consumer Society Reader*, New York: The New Press.

Bourdieu, Pierre (1984). *Distinction: A Social Critique of the Judgment of Taste*, Mass.: Harvard University Press.

Braudel, Fernand (1979). *The Structures of Everyday Life*, New York: Harper & Row.

Bremmer, Jan and Herman Roodenburg (eds) (1991). *A Cultural History of Gesture*, Oxford: Polity.

Brillat Savarin, Jean-Anthelme (1825/1970). *The Physiology of Taste*, New York: Liveright.

Brookes, Maureen (2004). "Shaping Culinary Taste: the Influence of commercial operators (We are what we eat, or what we are persuaded to eat?)", in Donald Sloan (ed.), *Culinary Taste: Consumer Behaviour in the International Restaurant Sector*, Oxford: Elsevier Butterworth-Heinemann.

Brown, Richard Harvey (2003). "Narration and Postmodern Mediations of Western Selfhood", in Richard Harvey Brown (ed.), *The Politics of Selfhood*, Minneapolis: Minnesota University Press.

Bruni, Frank (2008). "To Dine at Momofuku Ko, First You Need Nimble Fingers", in the *New York Times*, 7 May.

Burnett, John (2004). *England Eats Out: A Social History of Eating Out in England from 1830 to the Present*, Edinburgh: Pearson Longman.

Burney, Fanny (1778). *Evelina*, Public Domain: Kindle.

Butler, Judith (1990). *Gender Trouble*, New York: Routledge.

———— (2005). *Giving an Account of Oneself*, New York: Fordham University Press.

Caillois, Roger (1961). *Man, Play and Games*, New York: Free Press.

Calvino, Italo (1979). *Invisible cities*, London: Pan.

Castle, Terry (1986). *Masquerade and Civilisation*, Palo Alto, CA: Stanford University Press.

———— (1987). "The Culture of Travesty: sexuality and masquerade in eighteenth century England", in G.S. Rousseau and Roy Porter (eds), *Sexual Underworlds of the Enlightenment*, Manchester: Manchester University Press.

Certeau, Michel de (1984). *The Practice of Everyday Life*, Trans. Steven Rendall, Berkeley, CA: University of California.

Chatwin, Bruce (1977). *In Patagonia*, London: Cape.

Clapp, Jennifer (2012). *Food*, Oxford: Polity.

Cleland, John (1748). *Memoirs of a Woman of Pleasure* (1999), New York: Oxford World Classic.

Congreve, William (1692). *Incognita*, Middlesex: Echo Library.

Costello, Diarmuid and Dominic Willsdon (eds) (2008). *The Life and Death of the Image*, New York: Cornell University Press.

Counihan, Carole and Penny Van Esterik (eds) (1997). *Food and Culture*, New York: Routledge.

Darnton, Roger (1984). *The Great Cat Massacre*, New York: Basic.

David, Elizabeth (1969/1998). *Italian Food*, London: Penguin.

Debord, Guy (1977). *The Society of the Spectacle*, Online: Black and Red.

DeFoe, Daniel (1719). *Robinson Crusoe* (2003), London: Penguin Classics.

——— (1722). *The Fortunes and Misfortunes of the Famous Moll Flanders* (1989), London: Penguin Classics.

de Waal, Edmund (2010). *The Hare with Amber Eyes: A Hidden Inheritance*, London: Chatto & Windus.

Douglas, Mary (1972). *Purity and Danger: An Analysis of Concepts of Pollution and Taboo*, London: Routledge and Kegan Paul.

——— (1979). "Les structures du culinaire", *Communications* 31: 145–70.

du Gay, Paul (2007). *Organizing Identity*, London: Sage.

Eagleton, Terry (1998). *The Eagleton Reader*, S. Regan (ed.), Oxford: Blackwell.

Eco, Umberto (1973). "Social Life as Sign", in D. Robey (ed.), *Structuralism*, Oxford: Oxford University Press.

——— (1986). *Travels in Hyperreality*, New York: Harcourt Brace & Co.

Elias, Norbert (1939/1978). *The Civilizing Process*, New York: Urizen.

——— (1982). *Power and Civility*, New York: Pantheon.

Erickson, Karla (2007). "Tight Spaces and Salsa-stained Aprons: Bodies at Work in American Restaurants", in David Beriss and David Sutton (eds), *The Restaurants Book: Ethnographies of Where We Eat*, Oxford: Berg.

Esterl, Mike (2013). "Fizzy drink revenue falls flat as consumers kick the habit", *Wall Street Journal International*, 22 January.

Felski, Rita (1995). *The Gender of Modernity*, Mass.: Harvard University Press.

Fielding, Henry (1741). *An Apology for the Life of Mrs Shamela Andrews*, Online: Free Books.

Fine, Ben (ed.) (1998). *The Political Economy of Diet, Health and Food Policy*, London: Routledge.

Fine, Gary Alan (1996). *Kitchens: The Culture of Restaurant Work*, Berkeley, CA: University of California.

Finkelstein, Joanne (1989). *Dining Out: A Sociology of Modern Manners*, Oxford: Polity.

Fisher, M.F.K. (1954). *The Art of Eating*, New York: World Publishing.

Flammang, Janet A. (2010). *The Taste of Civilization: Food, Politics and Civil Society*, Urbana, IL: University of Illinois.

Foer, Jonathan Safran (2009). *Eating Animals*, London: Hamish Hamilton/Penguin.

Forster, E.M. (1980). *A Room with a View*, London: Penguin Classics.

Foucault, Michel (1978). *Discipline and Punish*, New York: Vintage.

——— (1983). *History of Sexuality: Care of the Self*, Vol. 3, London: Penguin.

Freud, Sigmund (1900). "The Interpretation of Dreams", Trans. James Strachey (ed.), *The Standard Edition of the Complete Psychological Works of Sigmund Freud*, London: Hogarth Press 1952–74, Vol. 4.

Furetière, Antoine (1708/1978). *Dictionnaire Universel*, Paris: Parmentier.

Garber, Marjorie (1992). *Vice Versa*, New York: Penguin.

Geertz, Clifford (1983). *Local Knowledge*, New York: Basic.

Gill, A.A. (2012). "What's wrong with the Michelin Guide? Everything", *Vanity Fair*, November 2012.

Goethe, J.W. (1774/1989). *The Sorrows of Young Werther*, London: Penguin Classics.

Goffman, Erving (1961). *The Presentation of Self in Everyday Life*, New York: Doubleday.

——— (1969). *Strategic Interaction*, Pennsylvania: University of Pennsylvania Press.

Goldman Robert and Stuart Papson (1996). *Sign Wars*, New York: Guilford.

Gombrich, Ernst (1960). *Art and Illusion*, London: Phaidon.

Goody, Jack (1982). *Cooking, Cuisine and Class*, Cambridge: Cambridge University Press.

Gottdiener, Mark (2001). *The Theming of America*, Boulder, CO: Westview.

Graves, Robert (translator) (1951). *The Golden Ass (or Lucius Apuleius)*, New York: Farra, Straus and Giroux.

Greenblatt, Stephen (1980). *Renaissance Self-Fashioning*, Chicago, IL: University of Chicago.

——— (2004). *Will in the World: How Shakespeare became Shakespeare*, New York: Norton.

Griffiths, Sian and Jennifer Wallace (eds) (1998). *Consuming Passions: Food in the Age of Anxiety*, Manchester: Manchester University Press.

Gronow, Jukka (1997). *The Sociology of Taste*, London: Routledge.

Gustafson-Larson, A.M. and R.D. Terry (1992). "Weight-related behaviors and concerns of fourth-grade children", *Journal of the American Dietetic Association* 92 (7): 818–22.

Harp, Stephen L. (2002). "The Michelin Red Guides: Social differentiation in Early-Twentieth-Century French Tourism", in Rudy Koshar (ed.), *Histories of Leisure*, Oxford: Berg.

Head, Simon (2003). *The New Ruthless Economy: Work and Power in the Digital Age*, Oxford: Century Foundation, Oxford University Press.

Hebdige, Dick (1993). "A Report from the Western Front: postmodernism and the "politics" of style", in Chris Jenks (ed.), *Cultural Reproduction*, London: Routledge, pp. 69–103.

Hubbert, Jennifer (2007). "Serving the Past on a Platter: Cultural Revolution Restaurants in Contemporary China", in David Beriss and David Sutton (eds), *The Restaurants Book: Ethnographies of Where We Eat*, Oxford: Berg.

Huizinga, Johann (1949). *Homo Ludens: A Study of the Play Element in Culture*, London: Routledge and Kegan Paul.

Hunt, Lynn (ed.) (1993). *The Invention of Pornography: Obscenity and the Origins of Modernity 1500–1800*, New York: Zone.

Illouz, Eva (1997). *Consuming the Romantic Utopia*, Berkeley, CA: University of California.

——— (2007). *Cold Intimacies*, Oxford: Polity.

Inglis, Fred (2010). *A Short History of Celebrity*, New Jersey: Princeton University Press.

James, Henry (1881). *A Portrait of a Lady*, London: Penguin Classics.

Kafka, Franz (1915). *The Metamorphosis*, Online: Kessinger reprint.

Kemp, Martin (2012). *Christ to Coke: How Image Becomes Icon*, Oxford: Oxford University Press.

Lang, T. and M. Heasman (2004). *Food Wars: The Global Battle for Mouths, Minds and Markets*, London: Earthscan.

Langman, Lauren (1992). "Neon Cages: Shopping for Subjectivity", in Rob Shields (ed.), *Lifestyle Shopping: The Subject of Consumption*, London: Routledge.

Langman, Lauren and Maureen Ryan (2009). "Capitalism and the Carnival Character: the escape from reality", *Critical Sociology* 35 (4): 471–92.

Lavater, Johann Caspar (1885). *Essays on Physiognomy*, Trans. T. Holcroft, London: Ward, Lock and Bowden.

Lawrence, Felicity (2010). "Defra's joined-up thinking recognises the fragility of UK food Production", *Guardian*, 5 January 2010.

Le Rider, Jacques (1993). *Modernity and the Crises of Identity*, Oxford: Polity.

Levenstein, Harvey (1988). *Revolution at the Table: The Transformation of the American Diet*, New York: Oxford University Press.

—— (2003). *Paradox of Plenty: A Social History of Eating in Modern America*, Berkeley, CA: University of California.

Lévi-Strauss, C. (1969). *The Raw and Cooked*, New York: Random House.

—— (1978). *The Origins of Table Manners*, New York: Harper and Row.

Lingis, Alphonso (1994). *Abuses*, Berkeley, CA: University of California Press.

Lynes, Russell (1949). "Highbrow Lowbrow, Middlebrow", in *Harper's Magazine*, February: http://harpers.org/archive/1949.

MacCannell, Dean (1989). *The Tourist: A New Theory of the Leisure Class*, New York: Schocken.

MacDonald, Dwight (1944). "A Theory of Popular Culture", *Politics 1*, no. 1, February pp. 20–3.

MacKenzie, Henry (1771). *A Man of Feeling* (1987), Brian Vickers (ed.), Oxford: Oxford University Press.

Magli, Patricia (1989). "The Face and the Soul", in M. Feher, R. Naddaff and N. Tazi (eds), *Fragments for a History of the Human Body*, Mass.: Zone.

Mars, Gerald and Michael Nicod (1984). *The World of Waiters*, London: Allen and Unwin.

Martin, Raymond and John Barresi (2006). *The Rise and Fall of Soul and Self*, New York: Columbia University Press.

Mayle, Peter (1991). *A Year in Provence*, New York: Random.

Mennell, S. (1985). *All Manner of Food*, Oxford: Blackwell.

Mills, C.W. (1951). *White Collar*, New York: Oxford University Press.

Mintz, Sidney (1985). *Sweetness and Power*, New York: Penguin.

———— (1996). *Tasting Food, Tasting Freedom: Excursions into Eating, Culture and the Past,* Boston, MA: Beacon.

———— (1997). "Time, Sugar and Sweetness", in Carole Counihan and Penny van Esterik (eds), *Food and Culture,* London: Routledge.

Mitchell, W.J.T. (2004). *Cloning Terror,* Chicago, IL: University of Chicago.

Nestle, Marion (2002). *Food Politics: How the Food Industry Influences Nutrition and Health,* Berkeley, CA: University of California.

Norman, B. (1972). *Tales of the Table: A History of Western Cuisine,* New Jersey: Prentice Hall.

Packard, Vance (1957). *The Hidden Persuaders,* Berkeley, CA: University of California.

Pardue, Derek (2007). "Familiarity, Ambience and Intentionality: An Investigation into Casual Dining Restaurants in Central Illinois", in David Beriss and David Sutton (eds), *The Restaurants Book: Ethnographies of Where We Eat,* Oxford: Berg.

Paules, Greta Foff (1991). *Dishing It Out: Power and Resistance Among Waitresses in a New Jersey Restaurant,* New Jersey: Princeton University Press.

Peakman, Julie (2004). *Lascivious bodies: A Sexual History of the Eighteenth Century,* London: Atlantic.

Pesman, Ros (1996). *Duty Free: Australian Women Abroad,* Oxford: Oxford University Press.

Pillsbury, Richard (1990). *From Boarding House to Bistro: The American Restaurant Then and Now,* Boston, MA: Unwin Hyman.

Porter, Roy (ed.) (1997). *Rewriting the Self,* London: Routledge.

———— (1982). *English Society in the Eighteenth Century,* London: Penguin.

———— (2000). *London: A Social History,* London: Penguin.

Portús, Javier (2012). "Paintings in Spain 1550–1900", in *Portrait of Spain,* Prado: Madrid.

Potter, Dennis (1986). *The Singing Detective,* London: Faber.

Raban, Jonathan (1974). *Soft City,* London: Hamilton.

Rabobank (2000). World Markets for Organic Fruit and Vegetables [Online] Available at: www.fao.org/docrep/004/y1669e/y1669e00.htm [accessed 16 May 2012].

Rebora, Giovanni (2001). *The Culture of the Fork,* New York: Columbia University Press.

Revel, J-F. (1982). *Culture and Cuisine,* New York: Doubleday.

Richardson, Samuel (1740). *Pamela or Virtue Rewarded*, Online: Forgotten Books (2008).

Richter, Simon (2002). "Food and Drink: Hegelian encounters with the culinary other", in Alison Phipps (ed.), *Contemporary German Cultural Studies*, London: Arnold.

Ripe, Cherry (1993). *Goodbye Culinary Cringe*, Australia: Allen & Unwin.

Ritzer, George (1996). *The McDonaldization of Society*, Thousand Oaks, CA: Pine Forge Press.

—— (ed.) (2002). *McDonaldization: The Reader*, Thousand Oaks, CA: Pine Forge Press.

Root, Waverley (1958). *The Food of France*, London: Cassell.

Rorty, Richard (1989). *Contingency, Irony, Solidarity*, Cambridge: Cambridge University Press.

Rose, Nikolas (1996). *Inventing Our Selves*, Cambridge: Cambridge University Press.

Rousseau, G.S. and Roy Porter (eds) (1987). *Sexual Underworlds of the Enlightenment*, Manchester: Manchester University Press.

Schama, Simon (2004). *Hang-ups: Essays on Painting (Mostly)*, London: BBC Books.

Schlosser, Eric (2002). *Fast Food Nation*, London: Penguin.

Sennett, Richard (1976). *The Fall of Public Man*, Cambridge: Cambridge University Press.

—— (1994). *Flesh and Stone: The Body and the City in Western Civilization*, London: Faber and Faber.

Seth, Vikram (1983). *From Heaven Lake*, London: Chatto & Windus.

Sharpe, Kevin and Steven Zwicker (eds) (2008). *Writing Lives*, Oxford, Oxford University Press.

Simmel, Georg (1900/1990). *The Philosophy of Money*, Trans. Tom Bottomore, London: Routledge.

—— (1905/1971). "The Metropolis and Mental Life and Sociability", in David Levine (ed.), *On Individuality and Social Forms*, Chicago, IL: University of Chicago.

—— (1950). *The Sociology of Georg Simmel*, Chicago, IL: University of Chicago.

Sloan, Donald (ed) (2004). *Culinary Taste: Consumer Behaviour in the International Restaurant Sector*, Oxford: Elsevier Butterworth-Heinemann.

Sontag, Susan (1964). *Against Interpretation*, New York: Farrar, Straus & Giroux.

——— (1973). *On Photography*, New York: Farrar, Straus & Giroux.

Spang, Rebecca (2000). *The Invention of the Restaurant: Paris and Modern Gastronomic Culture*, Mass.: Harvard University Press.

Spradley, James and Brenda Mann (1975). *The Cocktail Waitress*, Illinois: Waveland Press.

Steinberger, Michael (2010). *Au Revoir to All That: The Rise and Fall of French Cuisine*, London: Bloomsbury.

Stern, Jane and Michael (1978/2002). *Roadfood*, New York: Broadway Books.

Sterne, Laurence (1759). *The Life and Opinions of Tristram Shandy, Gentleman*, Public Domain: Kindle.

Stone, Lawrence (1972). *The Causes of the English Revolution 1529–1642*, London: Routledge and Kegan Paul.

Taylor, Charles (1989). *Sources of the Self: The Making of Modern Identity*, Cambridge: Cambridge University Press.

Taylor, Paul and Jen Harris (2008). *Critical Theories of Mass Media*, Berkshire, England: Open University Press McGraw Hill.

Thomas, Keith (2009). *The Ends of Life: Roads to Fulfillment in Early Modern England*, Oxford: Oxford University Press.

Todd, Janet (1986). *Sensibility: An Introduction*, London: Methuen.

Töennies, F. (2001). *Community and Civil Society*, Cambridge: Cambridge University Press.

Trubek, Amy (2007). *The Taste of Place*, California: University of California.

Trumbach, Randolph (1987). "Modern prostitution and gender in Fanny Hill: libertine and domesticated fantasy", in G.S. Rousseau and Roy Porter (eds), *Sexual Underworlds of the Enlightenment*, Manchester: Manchester University Press.

Varriano, John (2009). *Taste and Temptations: Food and Art in Renaissance Italy*, California: University of California Press.

Venturi, Robert, Denise Scott Brown and Steven Izenour (1977). *Learning from Las Vegas*, Mass.: MIT.

Wahrman, Dror (2004). *The Making of the Modern Self*, New Haven, CT: Yale University Press.

Whyte, W.F. (1948). *Human Relations in the Restaurant Industry*, New York: McGraw-Hill.

Wilde, Oscar (1966). *The Picture of Dorian Gray*, Harmonds: Penguin.

Williams, Raymond (1961). *The Long Revolution*, Harmonds: Penguin.

Williams, Rosalind (1982). *Dream Worlds: Mass Consumption in Late Nineteenth Century France*, Berkeley, CA: University of California.

Wittgenstein, Ludwig (1980). *Remarks on the Philosophy of Psychology*, Oxford: Blackwell.

———— (1980). *Culture and Value*, Trans. Peter Winch. Oxford: Blackwell.

Wood, R.C. (1995). *The Sociology of the Meal*, Edinburgh: Edinburgh University Press.

Xiaolong, Qiu (2004). *When Red is Black*, London: Hodder & Stoughton.

Young, Patrick (2002). *"La Vieille France* as Object of Bourgeois Desire: The Touring Club de France and the French Regions, 1890–1918", in Rudy Koshar (ed.), *Histories of Leisure*, Oxford: Berg.

FILMS

Babette's Feast (1987). Directed by Gabriel Axel. Denmark: Panorama A/S.

Catfish (2010). Directed by Ariel Schulman and Henry Joost. USA: Rogue.

Chocolat (2000). Directed by Lasse Hallstrom. USA, France: Miramax.

The Cook, the Thief, his Wife and her Lover (1989). Peter Greenaway. UK, France: Miramax.

Food Inc. (2008). Directed by Robert Kenner. USA: Magnolia Pictures.

Last Tango in Paris (1972). Directed by Bernardo Bertolucci. France/ Italy: United Artists.

Michelin Stars (2010). Directed and produced by Michael Waldeman. UK: BBC.

Pulp Fiction (1994). Directed by Quentin Tarantino. USA: A Band Apart.

Super Size Me (2004). Directed by Morgan Spurlock. USA: Kathbur Pictures.

Tampopo (1985). Directed by Juzo Itami. Japan: Itami Productions.

When Sally Met Harry (1989). Directed by Rob Reiner. USA: MGM.

INDEX